Out of the DARK
AND INTO GOD'S LIGHT

by

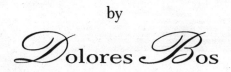

Dolores Bos

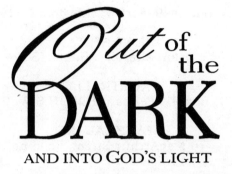

Out of the DARK

AND INTO GOD'S LIGHT

by

$Dolores$ Bos

CHRISTIAN • LITERATURE • CRUSADE
Fort Washington, Pennsylvania 19034

CHRISTIAN LITERATURE CRUSADE

U.S.A.
P.O. Box 1449, Fort Washington, PA 19034

GREAT BRITAIN
51 The Dean, Alresford, Hants., SO24 9BJ

AUSTRALIA
P.O. Box 91, Pennant Hills, N.S.W. 2120

NEW ZEALAND
10 MacArthur Street, Feilding

Edited by Robert Delancy

ISBN 0-87508-720-5

PRINTED IN THE UNITED STATES OF AMERICA

DEDICATION

This book is dedicated to
my husband Lawrence, Sr.,
and our family,
all of whom are
my special blessings.

Nancy Chapel
1975

INTRODUCTION

"As for you, you meant evil against me, but God meant it for good..."—Genesis 50:20.

THE story of Nancy Chapel is written here as a testimony to the infinite greatness of our God, and to the wondrous way that He can change even the hardest of hearts into a loving vessel of service. It is hoped that all who read this real-life drama will see that the love of Jesus Christ is eternal and immeasurable, and that the evil others bring into our lives ultimately serves God's purpose for our good and for His glory.

Nadia Chaplya, born in a small hamlet in the northern Ukraine on December 31, 1924, knew no such God, nor did she care to know Him. She often declared, "There is no God! What kind of God would let me live in such horror!" Yet God reached down to Nadia, claimed her as His child, and prepared her for a life of service for Him as His chosen messenger.

God chose Nadia to be His spokesperson as a missionary to Nigeria for twenty years. Preaching the gospel in Africa was a long, difficult road from a famine-riddled village in the Soviet Union and a tormented life as a prisoner of war in Germany, but God is in control of everything and in everything He has a purpose and design that ultimately leads to a life of service for Him.

CONTENTS

*Two school friends and
Nadia (right) in the Ukraine, 1941.*

1

BITTER BEGINNINGS

"Do you think Papa will come home to-night, Nadia? Ivan Dushko may catch him if he does! Will he take us to jail, too?" Four-year-old Boris Chaplya looked at his sister Nadia with anxious eyes, his voice trembling just a bit. Boris was clearly troubled by what little his young mind could understand of his family's plight.

The two of them had been out by the pond, watching the men haul in their fish-nets from the almost frozen water near their house in Soldativ, in the upper Ukraine. This year, 1931, had been a lean one because of tighter food controls imposed on the people by the Russian government. The villagers were out late to-night doing their best to increase the supply of salted fish for their families. Snow had begun to fall softly and the town's lanterns could be seen glowing in the fading light.

"Ivan won't take us to prison, Boris," reassured Nadia, "but he will take Papa if he sees him."

Ivan! Just the mention of that name sent shivers through the young Ukrainian girl. This man had been trouble for her family for so long!

Ivan Dushko, a big ruddy-faced town constable, was greedy, cruel, and very powerful in the village—a man that most feared and no one trusted. If he wanted something, he just took it! For some time now, he had tried to get the rich, fertile land of the Chaplya farm with its large, productive orchard. Nadia's father, Anton, would not sell it and thus far had resisted all of Ivan's threats. He had to hide from Ivan to keep out of jail.

Nadia, wise for her eight years, realized that it was about time for her father, Anton Chaplya, to come home for food and clothing. He had been hiding in the forest for nearly two weeks, and she knew he must need provisions by now.

"Trouble," thought Nadia, "always trouble. Why doesn't Ivan just leave us alone!"

As the pair neared their house, they could hear angry shouts coming from inside. Suddenly, the door of the Chaplya's cottage flew open and their older sister came running toward them.

"Nadia! Boris! They are taking Papa away in chains," sobbed Maria. Her slender body shook with fright as she pulled her coat around her.

There was no time for a reply. Ivan Dushko came through the door, dragging a reluctant Anton Chaplya toward the waiting wagon. Bound securely and red-faced with anger, Anton shouted back through the open door to his wife.

"Don't you ever give up my farm! Do you hear me, Oksana? Never give it to him! You'll deal with me when I get back if you do!"

The Chaplya house, like the surrounding cottages, was simply constructed of wood and mud bricks, and was white-washed rather than painted. It faced a large pond that provided them with water, fish, and reeds for their thatched roof.

The farm did boast of a well-cared-for orchard that surrounded the house. Anton, his wife Oksana, and the three children had planted the trees and carried water from the pond daily to care for the young cherry trees. Now it was a productive orchard, and it made Anton's property a tempting asset.

Ivan Dushko wanted that property badly! It had become an obsession for Ivan, and he tried in every way possible to get it away from Anton. The battle between the two men had raged for several years.

Anton Chaplya was not an easy man. He was often quarrelsome and abusive, a condition brought on many times by excessive drinks of vodka. His visits to his home to gather provisions were not always the happiest of occasions. But now the conflict was over. It was apparent that Ivan had won the first battle.

Oksana Chaplya stood framed in the doorway of the two-room cottage, a picture of anguish and despair as she watched her husband struggle with the large, powerful Ivan Dushko. How could she hold off these men who were certain to increase their demands for the farm? How would they survive when the summer provisions were gone? The storehouse was almost depleted of last year's harvest now. The wagon pulled away with more angry shouts from Anton Chaplya, resulting in a few body blows from Ivan to quiet the irate man in chains.

Nadia's mother did her best to comfort and reassure her three frightened children. A meager supper was eaten in silence, as no one dared voice their thoughts. The wood fire was carefully banked for the night and the four Chaplyas huddled together in the warm alcove over the cooking oven, each wondering what the next day would bring.

The days and weeks that followed were filled with terror for the Chaplyas. Ivan and his men paid nightly visits to the little cottage, each time shouting their threats and helping themselves to anything in sight. Nadia put on layers of three or four dresses in anticipation of the raids so that she would have at least one outfit to wear the next day. Sometimes, however, the brutal men tore the clothes off their backs. Oksana tried to hide some of their family possessions by burying them in the cherry orchard, but Ivan always managed to find what she had concealed.

Oksana was ordered to open all boxes and doors that had locks and Ivan took what he wanted. Still, Nadia's mother would not sign over the farm and land to him. There was no way out of their dilemma.

The numerous raids on their food supply meant that Nadia's mother would have to go out and beg for food to feed her children. She was a determined woman. She would take care of her family at any cost. She seemed to have the stamina of steel, always working, never too tired to do just a little more.

Oksana's husband had two brothers living on nearby farms in Soldativ, but they refused to help her in this plight. All of the relatives of Anton Chaplya were fearful of getting involved with his family—afraid of severe punishment, as Anton had been labeled a "prisoner of the government." Oksana and her children were shunned by the entire village.

Weeks turned into months and the Chaplyas barely held on. Finally there was news of Anton. He had been taken to a labor camp in the forests of Siberia, a place where few survived. Nadia's mother worked long and hard to keep her family alive. There were many days that she returned home as darkness fell with very little to show for her search for food and firewood. These were anxious times for the children, always worried about the safety of their mother.

A sad-faced Boris sat by the small fireplace, watching Nadia and Maria as the two girls cooked soup made from the few provisions that were left in the storehouse.

"When will Mama come home, Maria?" he finally asked.

"Soon, I hope, Boris. It's getting dark outside, and I'd feel better if she were home," replied his sister.

Boris turned his blond head back toward the warmth of the fire, trying to keep the tears from running down his cheeks. Worry and fear seemed to be constant companions of the Chaplya children.

Suddenly, there was pounding on the door of the cottage and shouts of "Open up in there!"

The children had been told never to unbolt the door to anyone while their mother was away. The bolt didn't matter, however, as three burly men, led by Ivan Dushko, split the wooden door with an axe and rushed into the room.

Screaming with fear, the three children ran toward each other, clinging together for safety.

"Get out!" ordered Ivan. "Right now! Take nothing with you. Out in the snow. Move!"

The children were half thrown, half pushed out of the door and into the freezing Ukrainian weather. They ran to the shelter of a small shed behind the house. Cracks in the siding let the blowing wind in and the shivering children huddled together in an effort to shut out the cold. They could hear the sound of boards being nailed across the doors and windows of their cottage and they knew there would be no way back into the shelter of the house after Ivan left.

This was the scene that Nadia's mother

saw when she returned home that night. The children were nearly hysterical with fright, and frozen to the bone. Oksana had read the edict that was nailed to their door. It stated plainly that no one in the village could feed or house the Anton Chaplya family without suffering severe punishment.

From the house on the next farm, Stefan Chaplya had been watching the events at his brother's cottage. Stefan stood by the window staring into the night, trying to decide what he should do. He did not need to read the paper that was attached to the door. He knew what it said. He knew, too, that the threat of punishment was real. But how could he let his brother's children freeze to death before his very eyes!

His wife came up beside him. "Stefan, you cannot bring them in here! The authorities will kill you! Let them suffer for what your foolish brother did. It is no concern of ours!"

"Be quiet, woman!" commanded her husband. "I care nothing for my brother's wife, but those are Anton's children in that shed. How can I not help them?"

"We have very little food left, Stefan, certainly not enough to feed four more mouths. Think of what will happen should the authorities find out that we took them in." There was no sign of warmth or compassion in the eyes of his wife as she pleaded with her husband.

Reluctantly, Stefan Chaplya reached for his coat and started to the door. "No, Stefan, no! You cannot do this!"

The angry shouts of his wife were drowned out by the blowing of the harsh north winds as Stefan headed for his brother's shed. When he threw open the door he saw the three Chaplya children, wrapped in their mother's coat, shaking from fright and cold. Oksana looked at her brother-in-law, wondering what he was going to do. She did not completely trust him.

"Come with me to my house," he commanded. "You will die if you stay here."

Without waiting for a reply from Oksana, Stefan started back toward his house. His sister-in-law followed him through the blowing snow. Oksana was numbed by the cold and she did not relish the idea of going to Stefan's house, but she had to think of the children.

They received no open arms of concern as they entered the house, just stares of hatred from their uncle's family.

"Give them something warm to drink and show them where they can sleep."

This was all that anyone said.

Nadia Chaplya sat near the dying fire in the hearth, still shaken by what had happened to her. Her dark, curly hair clung in damp ringlets around her white face. She had seen no love in the face of Uncle Stefan's family as they came into the house. She knew that they were not wanted here. What was to become of them? Was there no one that cared?

Nadia's mother was exhausted beyond tears and was seated on the beaten dirt floor with Boris' head in her lap. "Where does she get the strength to keep going?" wondered Nadia. "Could it be from the icons of Joseph and Mary in the church?" On rare occasions, Nadia had gone with her mother to the Russian Orthodox Church and watched her mother as she knelt before the figures of the saints and prayed.

"What good did that do?" reflected Nadia. "We are worse off than ever now. The priest talked about 'God Almighty.' This was certainly not a God for the Chaplya family. If He was almighty, why would He let all of this happen to us?"

"There is no God! There is no one in all the earth that cares about us!" Tears slowly trickled down her small, thin face as she laid her head down on the rough mat that her uncle had given them as bedding. A tired Nadia fell into a deep sleep that released her from the concerns of what the morrow would bring.

Nadia's mother looked at her daughter and saw an exhausted child, a child that she knew was filled with fear and mistrust. There had been very little family life in the Chaplya household. Her husband drank too much. It had not been easy for Oksana to keep peace for long in the cottage, and she herself held a place of low esteem in the village because of Anton. Her children suffered from all of this, Nadia the most of all. Often Nadia acted as a go-between for her father and mother, not an enviable task for a young girl. She would try to console an angry Anton who had consumed too much vodka and at the same time protect Oksana from the blows of her irate husband.

Stalin, dictator of Russia, had orchestrated a severe famine in this region to bring the Ukrainians into submission to the Communist government. Truckloads of food sent to help the starving people were ordered dumped in the river. The ground was bare by the end of the summer, and the villagers often ate leaves and twigs just to keep alive. Nadia's own grandfather had died in their house of starvation. The old and the weak could not survive on such meager supplies. It was not uncommon to see a shrouded form being pulled on a sled to a burial ground.

Daily life in the village of Soldativ contributed to the atmosphere of fear that Oksana's children had to face. No one in the village dared speak his mind openly. There were informers paid by the government in even a family gathering, and punishment was swift and severe for speaking out against the Communist regime.

Oksana had watched Nadia withdraw within herself, daring not to love or trust anyone, but, rather, becoming bitter and resentful. What would become of her children? Hatred would be their companion and the future did indeed look bleak and difficult for Anton Chaplya's family.

And what if the police found them in Stefan's house? Oksana dared not think of the consequences. Stefan would surely be punished and Oksana would be blamed.

Oksana lay down beside her sleeping children and—realizing that she had no choice but to accept refuge in her brother-in-law's house—slept, and for the moment had rest from her turmoil.

2

HOMELESS AGAIN

"WOMAN!" the old man on the wagon shouted. "Your children look tired. You may ride to Rashevka on the hay in the back if you want."

Oksana Chaplya and her three children had been walking since early morning from Soldativ. Dusk was descending on the barren land of the upper Ukraine as the last rays of sun disappeared into thin layers of clouds hanging low to the ground. They had traveled six of the eight kilometers from Soldativ to Rashevka, quite a distance for small children to walk, but there was no other way to get to Rashevka, and they must find a place to live.

"Ride with us," offered the wife of the farmer. "It will be dark soon."

Grateful, Oksana lifted the children into the wagon. Young Boris clung close to his mother, still not sure of the events of the day. It was hard for him to understand why his aunt had demanded that they leave her house and never come back. They had been there for only a month. His small legs were tired and ached from walking on the uneven dirt roads, deeply rutted by the winter's wagon traffic. Maria quickly settled herself down in the soft hay, still looking defiant, making it clear that she needed no assistance from her mother. Maria had understood the quarrel between her mother and aunt early that morning and she was angry. Living with relatives who did not want you had been difficult for Maria. With this last situation in Uncle Stefan's house, indignation filled her features though her inner rage was punctuated by silence.

Oksana leaned against the side of the wagon and closed her eyes, trying to shut out the angry shouts from her sister-in-law that still echoed in her head as vividly as if she were back in that house facing the raging woman.

"My husband is dead, Oksana! You killed him," accused her sister-in-law. "It is your fault. He never should have brought you into this house. I told him to leave you out in the snow, but he wouldn't listen to me. Now they have killed him in prison for disobeying their edict. Leave, Oksana. You and your children! Leave this very day! I have no husband because of you, and you will not have the protection of my house!"

Nadia crept closer to her mother's side and Oksana reached out to pull her daughter's head down in her lap. Nadia, with her thin face framed by dark curls, always looked underfed and withdrawn. Oksana frequently offered her just a bit more than the other children. If there was an egg left, Nadia should have it.

"Mama, do we know anybody in Rashevka?" asked a sleepy Boris.

Oksana looked at him, wondering how to answer the little boy's question. "No, Boris," she finally said, "we know no one in Rashevka, but we will find a place to live. At least we are away from the unpleasantness of Uncle Stefan's house."

For the rest of the journey into Rashevka, mother and children slept, weary from the long day of walking. Oksana had brought a loaf of bread and some onions with her and this was the extent of their food. Each one carried a sack containing a few articles of clothing, not much more.

After Stefan's wife ordered Oksana out of her house, Oksana had quickly gone to her relatives' houses to collect the family possessions, kept safe for her after Ivan Dushko took over their house.

Oksana had brought to her marriage a dowry of good dishes, silverware and linens, and a few family heirlooms. She had been determined to save some of her valuables from Ivan Dushko's constant raids and had trusted her husband's relatives to keep them for her.

"What things, Oksana? We have nothing of yours. You are mistaken." Over and over, she heard these words. Doors slammed in her face as relatives refused to give back the few articles that Oksana had managed to keep from Ivan. She stood on their steps, tears forming in her eyes, and yet there was nothing she could do. Slowly, she turned back toward Stefan's house with a heavy heart.

"Just one more humiliation," sobbed Oksana to herself. "When will it ever end!"

Hastily, their possessions were put in sacks and the Chaplyas set out to walk to Rashevka. Where would they live? How would she find food for the children? Unanswered questions. But now, for the moment, exhausted Oksana slept in the farmer's wagon.

The abrupt braking of the wagon jolted the Chaplyas awake. "We are here in Rashevka," announced the farmer. "You must get out now."

Hastily, his passengers gathered their belongings and jumped from the wagon.

"Where do you go in Rashevka?" asked

the farmer's wife.

"I don't know," was Oksana's reply. "I must find a place to work for our food and shelter."

"Try the big farm down this road. They may have need of garden or field workers." With those parting words, the farmer and his wife continued on and left the four of them standing beside the muddy road on the outskirts of Rashevka.

Oksana and the children started off in the direction pointed out by the old woman. As they walked, Oksana looked around her. It had been a long time since she was in this town. Then, it was bright with fruit and sunflowers growing in profusion in the fields. The roads were crowded with farmers, all laden with stacks of fresh vegetables and newly picked cherries. But now, everything was deserted, dull and drab. The few people that passed seemed weighted down and bent over from the harsh life in the Ukraine.

"It is no better here," thought Oksana. "The famine has taken its toll on Rashevka as well as Soldativ."

The farm house that the woman on the wagon had pointed out to Oksana still had a lantern burning in the window.

"Stay here by the gate," requested

Oksana. It was best not to trust anyone too much these days in the Ukraine. The Communists had their spies everywhere and needed very little provocation to haul someone off to jail. Wandering about homeless was not accepted by these leaders, and Oksana feared she had revealed too much already to the old couple on the wagon. They were friendly enough, but could have been Communist informers. There was no way to know for sure.

The children, standing close to each other by the farmer's fence of woven vines, did as they were told and watched their mother walk up to the door of the house. No one answered her knock. She waited, and then slowly Oksana turned back toward the waiting children, but was stopped by a voice from the half open door behind her.

"What do you want?" the voice harshly demanded.

"I need a place for my children and me to stay in return for my work. Do you need help in the fields? Spring is not far off."

"Where is your husband, woman?"

"I have no husband. He is dead to us," replied Oksana. Again, Oksana feared she was revealing too much of their situation.

The man at the door looked at this

woman standing in front of him. She was small in stature with her dark hair covered by her scarf. Her face showed the struggles she had endured; lines revealed the accompanying worry and strain. But there was a look of determination in that face. "How much work can this small woman do?" he wondered.

"Wait here." The door closed and Oksana was left standing on the steps, not knowing what to expect. After a few minutes, the door opened again and the man told Oksana to go to the back of the house.

"There is a room you can use, and a stove for wood. I need field and garden help. I have very little food to give you. Be in the fields at dawn."

That was the beginning of three extremely hard years for this determined small woman and her children. Oksana worked from dawn to dark every day, drawing from a source of endless strength, eating only half of her lunch that was given the workers, bringing the remaining food home at night to three hungry children.

At times, Oksana walked to neighboring farms, looking for work when there was no work for her where they lived. She was sometimes gone for a week at a time, coming back to the one room to bring only a crust of bread and a few vegetables to her children. Oksana was paid for her labor in flour and other foods, but it was never enough. Often, when Nadia's mother had returned from working in the distant villages, thieves had broken in and had stolen what meager supplies they had. But Oksana still carried on, struggling from day to day to keep her family alive when it seemed that life was not worth saving.

"Nadia," Maria called to her younger sister, "we must go out and find food for ourselves. Mama will not be back for two days and we have nothing to eat."

"Where will we get food, Maria?" questioned Nadia, puzzled by her sister's request. "No one will let us work and we have no money to buy anything."

"Go to the door of a farmhouse and ask for food!" was the reply.

"You mean, beg?" Nadia's dark eyes were wide in amazement. "No, Maria! We cannot do that." Even in these difficult days, begging was shameful to the Chaplya family.

"Would you rather starve? Why should we go without when there is food nearby!"

"But, Maria, I can't do that!"

"Then starve, Nadia, there is no choice."

With those words thrown back by her

sister, Nadia was left alone in the room as Maria, with Boris in tow, walked out of the door to search for food.

Nadia stood there, wondering what to do. Maria was right, she eventually decided. If she needed food, she would have to go out and ask for it.

Nadia set out for the next farmhouse with knots in her stomach as she thought about asking for food from a stranger. As she approached the house, Nadia saw a woman coming out of a rickety barn behind the house carrying a sack of potatoes.

"Who are you?" demanded the woman, as she saw Nadia coming toward her. Her gruff tone did nothing to ease the fear inside of Nadia.

"I live down there," stammered the child, pointing down the road to the next farm. "Our mother is gone and we need food." The words tumbled out of Nadia's mouth as if she were trying to get the distasteful deed done.

"Get off of my land! I have no food for begging children!" With angry eyes the woman came toward Nadia. Nadia was terrified, as well as humiliated. She fled as fast as her legs would carry her.

"Never, never, never, will I beg again! If I starve and die, I will never do that again!" sobbed Nadia. She ran through the door to their one room and curled up in a corner, trying in vain to shut out the ugly world around her.

The Ukrainian people were very nationalistic and ambitious. But they had suffered a great deal at the hand of Stalin. The famine had not brought them to their knees as quickly as the dictator had thought. The people resisted the government's efforts to strip them of ownership of the land. All of the borders were still closed around the Ukraine and the people continued to suffer.

Crops of the summer came in very slowly because of the cold temperatures of the Ukraine, and the year's supplies ran out. People from the cities came to the rural sections of the country with their possessions to exchange them for food.

The Chaplya family was hungry, too. But they had nothing to exchange for food. Nadia and Maria walked many miles just to dig up rotten potatoes from a field, and these tasted like delicacies to the starving children.

In the end, Stalin had his way. Some of the people of the Ukraine had survived, but they had no interest nor energy to think about anything but food. Their spirit was broken and they did as they were told. Their farms were turned into collective enterprises, churches were converted into granaries, and most good books and Bibles were burned. The Communist government was determined to take away all that remained of the pride and education of the Ukraine, isolating the people from the truth and making them subservient to the Supreme Soviet. For the people of the Ukraine, the monstrous dictator Stalin had taken the spark of life from them; their belief in God, their freedom and their hope all were diminished.

Oksana clung fervently to her glimmer of hope and her inward faith, a faith that was not discussed or brought out into the light of day. She had brought her Bible with her from Soldativ, even though she knew that to be discovered possessing a Bible meant swift punishment—her life, perhaps. She never read it openly, but it was there, her cherished possession.

As for Nadia, there was no need to discuss God with her. She had no room in her heart for a God that would allow such unfairness and persecution, even the starvation of so many people. Her heart was full of hatred, fear, suspicion and despair. Why should she care if they burned the Bible? She was puzzled because her mother insisted on keeping that book in their house. Why believe? God must be keeping His love and goodness for other people, not Nadia, if indeed there was a God! Such thoughts continued to fill the entire being of Nadia Chaplya. There was no joy for her in life; only separation, being marked as an undesirable—the child of a political prisoner—and doomed to bear the scorn and hatred of others for the rest of her life.

3

TERROR IN SOLDATIV

"LOOK, Mama, the cherry trees are still there!" Nadia had run ahead of the others to catch the first glimpse of their cottage. "And the house is there, too. I see it!"

A smile spread over Oksana Chaplya's face as she heard the excited cries of her daughter. It had been eight years since she and the children had been forced to leave their house by the side of the pond in Soldativ, and she was relieved to find it still standing. Oksana had made the decision to return to Soldativ and their home when rumors reached her that the house was empty.

These same rumors that had told of the vacant house in Soldativ also suggested that her husband, Anton, had been released from the Siberian prison, but she dared not believe it. No word had come from Anton directly, and if it did she would plead with him to keep away from them. Oksana and the children had endured a great deal of persecution and shunning because of her husband's status as a political prisoner.

It was now the summer of 1941. The Communist officials who had ruled the Ukraine with an iron hand for a decade under the leadership of Joseph Stalin had been frightened into flight. This was because the German army had crossed the borders of the Ukraine in their quest to dominate all of Europe. Ivan Dushko, who had forced the Chaplyas out of their home eight years before, decided that working a farm and orchard was too difficult and not worth the trouble of dealing with the advancing Germans. He and his comrades left Soldativ to seek a softer life elsewhere.

This was the news that had reached Oksana in Rashevka. If it was true, they could go back to live in their old house again. As Oksana walked the eight kilometers from Rashevka to Soldativ with Nadia, Maria and young Boris, she hoped that she had made the right decision. The Ukraine was in a state of turmoil as the people tried to deal with the German troops who now occupied the area.

"But look, Nadia, under the trees!" Boris had come up beside her. "What's in there?" asked the puzzled boy as he stared into the orchard by the house.

A closer look revealed that there were two German tanks, camouflaged with brown and green paint, nestled among the green branches of those trees that Nadia and Maria had planted with their father, Anton, and tended daily with water from the pond many years ago.

War had come to Nadia's homeland. The presence of the tanks confirmed it. Soldativ, like the other neighboring villages, would have to live under the rule of a foreign power. German soldiers of Adolph Hitler's Third Reich had stormed through Poland and on into the Ukraine. The villagers had heard of the atrocities that were committed by the invaders in Kiev. Stories were told of Jewish people forced from their homes and killed or sent to concentration camps. The rural villages of the Ukraine were occupied as well by the Germans, but were not terrorized as were Kiev and other major cities. Jews were the Germans' primary target. It seemed as if the people of the Ukraine had exchanged Communist oppression for German brutality.

Nadia stood by the side of the road that led into Soldativ and looked in disbelief. Everywhere, fields were ripped apart, barns burned to the ground, wagons destroyed. Anything that could be of use had been ruined by the retreating Soviet forces as they fled the rapidly advancing

German army. They were determined to leave nothing intact for the invading troops to use. It was the same all along the road from Rashevka. Oksana, seeing the devastation, wondered if there would be any work in these torn-apart fields. Somehow they must find a way to get food and earn a living.

Life had become easier for the Chaplya family in Rashevka after Oksana found a job as janitor of the elementary school, but for Nadia, the same dark thoughts and suspicions had clung about her constantly. For her, all people were evil and bent on doing horrible things. She hung back from activities in school with the other students. Nadia was not willing to bear any more of their ridicule and scorn than necessary. She was the "undesirable child" of a political prisoner.

"Mama," asked Nadia of her mother one day as she cleaned the desks of the school, "why do other people have so much all of the time and we have so little? It doesn't seem fair." She often thought that there must be a special God for these people. It was clear to Nadia that she was not one of those privileged people, if there was such a God.

"Nadia, always tend to the needs of others first, and then to your own. Remember that," replied Oksana. This was not the first time that Nadia's mother had given her this advice. Oksana was convinced that it was the way to deal with the world and survive. But that was not an answer to Nadia's question.

Now, back in Soldativ, Nadia stood looking over the damaged fields. She asked the question again: "Why does this always happen to us, Mama. Are we that bad?"

Oksana turned to face her daughter, and saw the same look of despair that Nadia bore so often. How could she answer this?

"Nadia, I know that you are disappointed that you could not study anymore to be a teacher, but we have work to do to put our house in order. For now, just think about that."

Again, no answer for Nadia.

Nadia was indeed disappointed that her studies in Gadyach had come to an end. For the first time in her life, Nadia had thought that she could amount to something. She could become a teacher and help her mother earn a living for the family. The long walk from Rashevka to high school in Gadyach each day was no burden for Nadia. She saw it as a means to becoming someone of worth. Now, that light had been extinguished and darkness fell once again over the heart of Nadia Chaplya. This time it was war and Germans that took away her dream.

"Come," called their mother, "let's go inside and begin to put things in order." With those words, the four Chaplyas walked toward the house that faced the pond, the place that held so many moments of pain in the past for them. It belonged to them once more.

Nadia worked beside Maria, Boris and her mother every day as they helped to reclaim and plant the fields of the cooperative farms in the village. Everyone in Soldativ was required by the German commandant of the town to register for work. For Oksana, it was a way to supply food for their table. The Chaplyas obeyed the rules set down by the German commandant, but Oksana insisted that the girls and Boris avoid the German soldiers in the town at all times. "Just do what you are told and keep out of their way." They had food and a roof over their heads, and they stayed to themselves as much as possible.

In early May of 1943, Nadia's personal terror began. It started the day young Boris burst through the cottage door, calling for his mother and Nadia. Boris and Maria had been in the village and they stopped to read the latest orders that were placed on the notice board in front of the town hall.

"Mama, the mayor of our town has put up a list of the young people who must report to the officials to be examined by the German doctors." Boris was repeating the words that he had read, not fully understanding the impact of his message. "Nadia's name is on the list, Mama! What does she have to do?"

Oksana understood the message only too well. Once before the German commander of the region had told the mayor to choose a certain number of young people to be examined. Those that were declared healthy were taken away as work prisoners into Germany. Boris had escaped the list. He had long suffered with a hernia and the Germans were not interested in a weakling. Maria was too old and was married to a Ukrainian fighting at the front with the Soviet Union Army. Now, here was the edict again! This time, though, it meant that Nadia would have to obey the order. Oksana felt the cold, icy stabs of horror in her entire being.

"No! No! Not Nadia. Not my daughter!" Oksana buried her face in her long skirt, trying to shut out the dreadful words.

Nadia could not speak. She stared at

Maria. Finally she stammered, "Is this really true, Maria?"

Maria, who had tried to stop Boris from blurting out the news, looked at the shocked faces of her mother and sister. "Yes, it is true, Nadia. You must go for the examination. The German doctors will arrive here early tomorrow."

As night fell around Soldativ the following evening, the dreaded exam was over. Nadia sat looking into the glowing embers of the fireplace. It was still cool enough in early May to need some warmth from a smoldering flame. She shivered slightly and silently expressed the wish that the darkness would swallow her up and relieve her of this impending disaster. She tried not to think about the humiliating day at the hands of the German doctors. That was not possible. The images were still fresh in her mind.

There were thirty young people in the room with the Nazi solders that morning, some from Soldativ, some from Rashevka. They were separated male and female, and taken into another room where two doctors awaited them.

"Take off your clothes and line up in two rows." The first order was barked at them by an angry looking soldier. There were no robes, nothing to cover their naked bodies. No one seemed to care that they were human beings. Animals was more like it. They were poked and prodded over every inch of their bodies, in clear view of others in the room. They were roughly handled, with no regard for their person. The main concern of these German doctors was to weed out the ones that would present a medical problem on the work details in Germany and determine who would not be able to perform efficiently. They did not want to be bothered with sick Ukrainian people.

The day seemed as though it would never end. The young people had stood naked for hours, frightened and humiliated. Late in the afternoon, it was over and they were given orders of acceptance or rejection.

Nadia took her paper from the German soldier and looked at it. Clearly stamped across the form was "Accepted." On the bottom of the paper it stated, "Departure, May 27, 1943. One small suitcase allowed."

Oksana had cried at the news—tears of anguish of a mother who did not want to believe that her daughter had to go to Germany as a working prisoner. Maria and Boris were strangely quiet, trying not to add to the distress of Nadia and her mother.

Now it was silent in the house. Nadia could only hear the rapid beating of her own heart. What would she do? Would these people torture her or kill her? Would she ever get back to Soldativ and her family? Was there no help from anywhere? She felt so alone, so defiled by the hideous exam. Suddenly, the tears that had been suppressed all day came cascading down Nadia's cheeks. Her body shook with sobs so great that she could not control her anguish. There was no hope for her. Not even her dear mother, Oksana, could help her now. How would she face it all? The extreme cruelty of man, once again!

Oksana stood in the doorway watching her daughter. How could she comfort her?

"Nadia, there is nothing I can do to keep you from this dreadful thing. My heart aches for you and for me." Oksana sat down facing Nadia. "You must bear this out, but you must always keep yourself pure and not give in to the persuading words that are bound to come from lonely men in a distant country. You will never regret keeping to yourself and repelling their advances. You must be true to yourself, Nadia." Nadia looked at her mother and could only nod weakly in consent.

Nadia knew what her mother was trying

to say. She had seen the behavior of the German soldiers in Soldativ. She knew how they treated some of the foolish village girls who disobeyed their parents and sought out the company of the army men.

All of this to think about! Nadia had no idea where she would be taken or what kind of work she would be required to do. Was she strong enough to cope with what was ahead for her? Why was there never anyone to help her? Nadia felt the despair of being completely alone.

The two days until May 27 went swiftly, and soon it was time to walk to where a railroad car was being loaded with twenty-five young people bound for Germany and servitude. They had strict orders not to converse with their friends or relatives. No contact was allowed. Silence was demanded. Boris, Maria and Oksana stood behind the barrier watching the process. Oksana looked at her daughter in the slowly moving line, a line that was taking Nadia away from her. As Nadia came nearer to where she stood, Oksana dared to thrust a piece of paper into her daughter's hand. Nadia quickly put the paper into her pocket before the guard could see what her mother had done.

Hours later, as Nadia rubbed her aching legs, tired from standing in the boxcar so long, she remembered the note from Oksana. She took care not to be seen as she slowly took the slip of paper from her pocket. Maybe her mother had written down the name of someone in Germany or along the way that could help her. She must be careful with the paper. Eagerly, she unfolded the note. She stared at the words.

"What kind of help is this?" Nadia could not believe what she read. It was the Lord's Prayer that her mother had written out for her and risked her life to give to her daughter as she left Soldativ. In disgust, Nadia stuffed the paper back into her pocket and felt only emptiness as she rode through the dark night bound for Germany and the terrifying unknown.

4

IN THE ENEMY'S HOUSE

"DUMMKOPF!" Johann Gulker glared at the cow that had just kicked his milking stool across the barn floor. It was late afternoon and the young German boy was tired and weary. Tension always seemed to fill his heart these days as he and his family tried to live under the tyrannical rule of Adolph Hitler. Johann had had more than his share of that stress yesterday.

Yesterday had been an extremely difficult time for all of the Gulker family. There had been much to accomplish on their farm in the town of Hardinghausen, near Hamburg in northwestern Germany. They had worked from dawn to dusk, slaughtering the required number of pigs and preparing the meat. A quota of food had to be met to send to the German troops fighting on many fronts in Europe. But there were additional chores that must be done as well as the tiring job of cutting meat. There were cows to milk twice a day, milk containers to scrub till they were gleaming clean, and everything had to be made ready so that the milk wagon could pick up the day's produce and carry it to the processing plant.

Johann's father had died in 1941, two years ago, and the burden of running the farm had fallen on the shoulders of the three Gulker brothers. Gert, the oldest son, and Gerhard, two years younger, were now serving in the German army under a dictator whom they didn't understand nor trust. That left Johann, his mother, three sisters and an eleven-year-old brother to try to carry on the work on the homestead. Times were not easy for the Gulker family.

The Gulker's next-door neighbor, Bernd Maathuis, had been appointed overseer of the Gulker farm. He had joined the Nazi party and his assignment was to make sure that the Gulker farm produced its quota of meat and produce.

Tired, dirty, and hungry, the family had trudged toward the house the previous evening to wash and sit down to a warm meal of potatoes, ham and sandwiches.

As they began to eat their meal, there was an urgent knock at the door. Mama Gulker nodded to Johann and the boy got up to open the front door.

"Johann! Johann!" wailed the woman at the door, as she fell into the young man's arms. "My husband has been taken!"

Johann recognized the sobbing woman as the wife of the minister of a neighboring town church and a good friend of the Gulker family. His mother heard the distress of the woman and came up behind her son.

"Marta, what is it? What has happened? Come in the house quickly, Marta. We must be careful. Someone might be watching you and listening to what you are saying." Informers were always poking about, ready to report any infraction of Nazi rule or dissenting views.

Slowly, the story unfolded as Marta struggled to control her weeping.

"Wilhelm was so late coming home from the church. We began to worry. My sons and I went down the north road to look for him in case he had an accident or had lost a wheel from the wagon. When we got near the bridge, we saw the wagon standing empty and the horses just left loose and not tied. I could not imagine what had happened. As we stood there, bewildered, a farmer from across the road came out and told us that some soldiers had stopped Wilhelm and dragged him from the wagon. They said he had spoken against Nazi rule and must pay for his crime. They will surely kill him! I will never see him again! What can I do?"

"Did he talk against Hitler?" inquired Johann. "Do you know what he might have said?"

"Last Sunday, he was talking to some of the men of the church after the service and I was standing near. I heard him say, 'But Hitler is not the supreme authority, you know.' That must have been reported by someone, but who would do such a thing? Surely, not a church member!"

The poor woman began to cry again. Nothing would console her. Mama Gulker waited until her friend's tears subsided and then said to her, "Marta, stay here with us tonight. Maybe we can find out something in the morning."

"No, no, I must go back. Wilhelm may come home. I must be there. Thank you for the kindness, Geesken, but I must go back. My sons will worry if I do not return. I was so frightened. I had to come to you."

When the pastor's wife had left, Johann looked at his mother. "Mama," he stammered, "he won't be back, will he? It will be just like our neighbor Derk Hutten, won't it? They will kill him. Am I right, Mama?"

"Yes, Johann. I am afraid that you are right. Another good man. It seems so horrible."

Now, a day later, Johann had no patience for a stubborn cow. He was tired from a sleepless night and was greatly worried about Dominie Wilhelm. But there was work to be done whether he felt like it or not.

"Dummkopf!" he exclaimed again at the cow. "Stand still!" Finally, settled on the milking stool, Johann began the familiar milking process. His thoughts wandered to the situation around his hometown of Hardinghausen and in other parts of his native Germany.

"How long can this go on? Rules, food quotas, curfews, all enforced by Hitler's men! How could our countrymen be so swept up by Hitler and his ideas? For two years we have endured hardships and humiliations at every turn. My brothers are off fighting for a cause that they don't understand, risking their lives every day for a madman."

Geesken Gulker's two older sons now served in the German army, not by choice, but by the orders of Hitler. One of the brothers, Gerhard, had been taken prisoner several months ago and was now in an English detention camp. At least he was alive and would not have to fight again.

Mama Gulker would not allow 18-year-old Johann to join the Young Nazi Party. "He is needed at home in place of his brothers," she had told the authorities and, thankfully, it remained that way. So Johann was not forced to join the arrogant group of militant young people who used most of every Sunday to drill and to learn Nazism. This was something Geesken Gulker would not permit; Sunday was a day set apart. It was not a day to drill or work or fill your head with Nazi propaganda. Sunday should be devoted to worship and church attendance. Geesken Gulker did her best to keep it that way in her household.

"We Gulkers can't even make decisions concerning our own farm," thought Johann, as he finished the milking chores. "We send the best of our food to the soldiers and the Third Reich tells us how much we can keep!" Anger welled up in the young German once more.

Johann could remember many times working through the night with the shutters closed to keep the light from showing, slaughtering a pig to prepare it for the family. The meat quota for the army often left the Gulkers with meat shortages. This was one way to store up extra meat for the family. By dawn, everything was scrubbed, put away and cleaned. No trace of the night's activities could be found.

All of Germany was in turmoil. Things had not been the same since that terrible night in November of 1939 when hate-filled Nazi soldiers ransacked Jewish synagogues all over Germany, destroying sacred Jewish treasures, burning their Torahs and breaking all of the windows of the buildings. "Kristallnacht" left the German people in shock and, from that devastating day in November, the Germany that Johann loved was never the same. Jews were killed or imprisoned. Those that remained were required to wear the Star of David sewn on their garments, and the German population was ordered to do no business with Jews. They were forbidden to associate with Jewish people at any level.

Johann turned to look at Anton Baron, milking in the next aisle of the barn. Anton was from Poland, brought to the Gulker farm as a prisoner to work for the family after he was captured by the German army as they stormed through the countryside of Poland. Anton was a good man, a hard worker. Johann could not help but feel guilty when he remembered the terrible things that Nazi soldiers had done to Anton's countrymen and the deliberate starving of the Polish people to bring them into submission to the German invaders. Johann could see the bright blue patch with the white letters OST on the shirt of Anton, a badge that was required to be attached to the clothing of all war prisoners to keep them separate and instantly distinguishable. Not the Star of David, but still a label for a human as if to shout "Unclean!" It was late evening before the two men had finished the milking. The cool breeze of the spring dusk felt refreshing, blowing gently through the barn doors.

Suddenly, Johann was aware of someone standing near them and he looked up to see a slender, dark haired girl, holding a small suitcase in one hand and a piece of stale bread in the other.

"Who are you?" asked a startled Johann. "Where did you come from?"

The strange girl only stood and looked at him. "Didn't you hear me? I asked, Who are you?" Johann could see that this young woman was very much afraid of her surroundings but was also determined to keep that fear in check.

"She doesn't speak German, Johann. She can't answer you." The voice came from behind him and Johann turned to see Bernd Maathuis, their overseer and neighbor. "She is from the Ukraine and is a prisoner sent here to help on the farm and in the house."

Johann then remembered that Bernd had gone into town to get a prisoner of war as extra help. He had also brought back a wagon and two more horses.

"What can she do? She looks too thin and young to do much work," replied Johann somewhat scornfully.

"Your age, I believe, Johann. She can work as well as the rest of you. Your mother needs help in the house with the twins and chores, and you need another hand in the fields and barn. Her name is Nadia Chaplya."

"Anton," he called, as he turned toward the Polish man who had been standing quietly aside observing the scene, "you can help her understand orders until she can learn some of the language. You speak some Russian, I hear."

Nadia Chaplya looked at the two men who were obviously talking about her. She could not understand what they said. She just stood there, clutching the suitcase tightly, unwilling to let the only possessions she had leave her side. She was tired, hungry, and frightened beyond description.

There had been little sleep for Nadia in

the last four days, just a bewildering series of events that left her numbed. She and many of the young people from Soldativ had traveled endless hours in a railroad boxcar like cattle taken to market. An armed guard was stationed at each door and no one doubted their ability to use those guns on the frightened group.

They had first stopped in Kiev, and were herded into an abandoned warehouse to sleep for the night. Makeshift bunks were hastily constructed. They slept in rows like stacked lumber. There were tears from some of the girls, harsh language from the young men, but all spoke in hushed voices. There was no need to think of escaping. They were told that death awaited anyone who dared try such action. The next morning, they left for Poland to be indoctrinated and to be assigned to their work situation in Germany.

Nadia stared at the blue square of cloth with OST printed on it. She could hardly believe that she must sew this on her clothes and wear it at all times. But then, feeling inferior and worthless was a familiar emotion in the life of Nadia Chaplya. Long ago, she had discovered the extreme evil that men were capable of inflicting on human beings. The Nazi officer who stood before the group of Ukrainian young people looked arrogant and defiant. Nadia had listened to this man talk for almost an hour. As her attention wandered, she felt afresh the sharp stabs of homesickness.

"How I miss my mother," she thought. "She must be terribly worried about me." Nadia almost jumped in her seat as once again she remembered the sharp sounds of gunshots that had rung out earlier in the day. She shuddered, thinking of the two young men who had decided to make a break for freedom.

They had been warned of the consequences of escape. They had been told that they would be shot on sight and that their parents would likewise be shot at home as punishment for their disobedience. The Nazi soldiers kept their word. She and her friends had rushed to the door of the makeshift auditorium at the sound of gunshots. There, on the dirt road leading to town, lay the bodies of the two boys shot down in their tracks as they attempted to run into the nearby forest and hide. The group of young people were led out to where the boys lay and were forced to look at them. The message was clear. Don't try to run away. Nadia thought of the parents of these boys who would be hauled out of their homes and killed because of a desperate dash to freedom by their sons.

Tears stung her eyes. She envisioned her own dear mother in that situation. No, she would not try to run away. What was the use? She had no money, no papers, nowhere to go in a strange country. And she would not risk her family's lives. She could still see the tear-streaked face of Oksana Chaplya as she watched her daughter being forced into the awaiting railroad car last week in Soldativ. Resentment flooded over Nadia as she recalled the scene! How she hated these people for the evil they had brought to her life! Trust no one, love no one. All such emotions just lead to hurt over and over again.

"Nadia! Come!" The words spoken in Russian brought her back to the present. The Polish man had called to her, and he took her by the arm and led her into the building to begin life in the enemy's house.

•   •   •

The soft glow of the end of a summer day spread a golden hue over the German farm and fields. Cut hay lay in sheaths on the ground, ready for the wagon that Johann and Nadia would drive again tomorrow. Nadia stood looking at the tranquil land and wondered what was happening to her.

She had been in the Gulker house for a little more than a year. To Nadia's amazement, she had not been beaten or mistreated, nor forced to work any harder than the rest of the family. The family had helped her learn the routine of the farm. Brother Jan had showed her how the family wanted their shoes polished, and young Fenna helped her with the haying— the drying, turning over and packing of the sheaves. Johann worked with her in the fields, showing her how to harvest the potatoes and other produce and the way she should care for the livestock. She learned how to cut meat, make sausages, and then scrub the equipment spotlessly clean. There was no task that Nadia refused to try, and eventually she mastered anything that she was asked to do. And in the process, she learned to understand and speak many German words. Nadia always stayed with her job until it was completed, never complaining about the hard work or long hours. Nadia had worked hard, doing her best.

She was always loyal to the family, never gossiping behind their backs. Nadia could sense that Mama Gulker liked her attitude toward her work and had begun to regard Nadia as a person, not just a servant, and certainly not as a war prisoner.

For Nadia, this was hard to accept. Part of her heart wanted to embrace the kindness of this family, to enjoy the trust that they all seemed to have in her. But the old, distrustful part of Nadia's makeup still resisted and pulled her back into her dark corner.

In the Gulker household there was laughter and an air of security and contentment. How could this be so? Their country was at war. Johann's brothers were fighting as German soldiers and in danger every day. She was their enemy, but the family did not treat her with malice or anger. Instead, she was allowed to be a part of the family, to gather by the stove in the great kitchen during the cold months and listen to the family talk together, join in with their fun, watch the children study their lessons for school and even hear them memorize lessons from their church, called "catechism." Such tenderness between the family members! Nadia had never seen this before! No suspicious attitudes or selfishness. It was all a mystery to Nadia. How did they dare lay themselves open to hurt by displaying their inner feelings to each other? If the truth was told, Nadia had begun to feel comfortable in this German household. She didn't understand it, but there was an attitude of peace and contentment—and Nadia wanted to hang on to that feeling.

Now, Nadia stood looking out at the tranquil scene from her bedroom window and reflected on the events of that morning. She and Johann had been in the field gathering the sheaves of hay that had been cut and made ready for storing in the barn. Nadia rode on top of the wagon, stacking the hay as Johann threw the bundles up to her. The horses kept up an even pace and the two young people worked steadily to get the job done.

Suddenly the weight of the load shifted, and Nadia and half of the load came tumbling down on the ground. Johann stopped the horses as quickly as he could and ran back to where Nadia lay beneath the hay.

"Are you hurt, Nadia? Are you all right?" inquired a worried Johann.

"Stay away from me. Stay away!" screamed Nadia. "You are trying to kill me!"

Johann could not believe what he was hearing. He thought they had reached a degree of mutual respect in the past year.

They had worked in the field together, milked cows daily together, and he was sure that she had begun to trust him as well as the rest of the family. But now she accused him of trying to kill her!

"What nonsense, Nadia! You know I did not try to kill you. You must know better than that!" declared a puzzled Johann.

"Just stay away. I am all right." Nadia scrambled to her feet and immediately began to gather the hay up from the broken bundles. She had been surprised herself at the outburst. The hatred that had surfaced so quickly left her embarrassed and bewildered.

"No, Nadia, that is not enough! Why do you accuse me of wanting to kill you? I don't understand at all!" Johann stood and looked straight at the frightened girl, waiting for a reply.

Nadia was shaking, ashamed that she had reacted in such a violent way to a very simple accident. The words had just flown out of her mouth.

"Johann," Nadia slowly replied, "I still have thoughts deep within me that tell me to trust no one. I have been afraid for so long! Everyone seems to be my enemy. Maybe someday this terrible darkness will be gone and I will not believe that people are still holding a gun to my head in hatred or disgust." With her eyes toward the ground, not daring to see the look in the young man's eyes, Nadia added, "I am sorry, Johann. Of course you meant me no harm."

Nadia was still not willing to trust anyone. Would she ever be able to laugh and be happy like this family? She was desperately lonely for her own family, and yet the Gulkers possessed something that she had never experienced in her own house in the Ukraine.

"Nadia. Nadia! Komm mit mir in die Kuche."

The familiar call brought Nadia back to the present. Mama Gulker was calling for her to help with getting supper on the table for the family.

As was her habit, Nadia responded at once and hurried toward the big kitchen to help put the steaming hot dishes of ham and potatoes with freshly sliced homemade bread on the table.

"Quickly, Nadia," ordered Mrs. Gulker. "The family is hungry."

Nadia did not have to be reminded that the Gulkers would be hungry! She had seen them at mealtime enjoying the plain fare set before them, never complaining about the lack of variety or the absence of some special meat dish, but just glad to be with their brothers and sisters and at Mama Gulker's table.

When the dishes were all set on the long wooden table, Mama rang the copper supper bell. Nadia helped the seven-year-old twins, Hanni and Frieda, into their chairs and then turned to go back into the kitchen to eat her meal with Anton and the other workers.

Nadia stopped at the doorway and turned to look at the gathered family. Johann was praying, and even the little children bowed their heads in reverence. Nadia observed them do this every time food was placed before them. She watched them read the Bible at the end of each meal and sometimes join hands and sing the psalms that the children memorized each week. Their voices, young and old, blended into one united praise to God the Father.

"Why do they do this?" wondered Nadia. "Nothing changes. Where is this God that hears these prayers? Is it the same God that my mother talked to on her knees before the icons in the Russian Orthodox Church at home?"

But this praying of the Gulker family was different. It sounded so personal. Nadia knew no such God. Nowhere did she see such a God. Evil spread its ugliness over the land and over people in Germany, in Russia, and in the Ukraine. As far as she could tell, praying like the Gulker family did changed nothing.

Every Sunday she helped to load up the Gulker's wagon with food for the day. The entire Gulker family climbed in and headed for a rented room in the neighboring town of Uelsen to spend the day attending church, eating their meals and visiting with friends and relatives. They returned at dusk and always they came home singing. What a mystery!

Nadia's German had improved rapidly. She knew the German alphabet from grade school classes in Rashevka and her reading ability was progressing.

"Maybe I should ask Mama Gulker for some children's books from their church and see if I can find out what makes this family different," thought Nadia. "Could it just be that it would help this heaviness I feel in my heart? Could there be joy somewhere for me, too?"

*The Gulker family
with Nadia.*

Herr Gulker's farm and dairy.

5

CHOSEN BY GOD

THE cool shade of the forest fell around
Nadia Chapyla. Tall trees gave her the
much needed relief from the hot afternoon sun. The cows were contentedly
grazing around the trees, savoring the
sweet grass of mid-summer in Germany.
The book in Nadia's hand captured her
whole attention and all seemed serene
that afternoon.

Nadia stopped reading to look at the
cattle, and seeing that all was well she sat
down on a fallen log. Every afternoon it
was her job to bring the Gulker cows out
to the fresh grass to graze. This was
Nadia's favorite place to think and relax.
Often she sat here to absorb the books
that Mama Gulker had given her to read.

Mrs. Gulker had been very pleased
when Nadia inquired about the church
books.

"Of course, Nadia. You are welcome to
read the books. I will select the ones I
believe will help you. It is good that you
have an interest in things about God. You
must read and learn, but you also must

let your heart listen to what your mind is learning. Talk with me about what you read and I will gladly help you understand about God and His creation."

Nadia breathed deeply of the fresh scent of the forest and then let out a long sigh, almost a contented sigh. She leaned back against the smooth bark of "her tree" and closed her eyes. So much had happened in the last month. It was hard to think of it all.

The books that she had read did speak to her heart. The words had given her a feeling of urgency, compelling her to read more and more of the stories about God and His promise of salvation to His children. She read about the God that she had denied for so long. Why was it different this time? Mama Gulker explained it as "the Holy Spirit working in your heart, making way for Him in your life, Nadia." Nadia liked to refer to Mrs. Gulker as "Mama," for indeed Geesken Gulker had come to think of this young girl from the Ukraine as one of the family. Geesken Gulker herself had suggested that Nadia call her "Mama," a gesture that greatly pleased a young woman so far away from her home and family.

The war that had engulfed much of the world was over now. Adolph Hitler had been killed in the battle of Berlin, choosing to die in a bunker rather than face disgrace as a fallen and defeated dictator.

Gert, the oldest Gulker son, had returned from Italy to a grateful family, and Gerhard would be home soon from the English prison. Johann had served for a time in the German army, and he too was at home once more. The family was together and thankful that none of the sons had suffered injuries or death.

The end of the war changed everything for Nadia Chaplya. She was no longer a prisoner of the Germans, but she was a long way from home in the Ukraine. Temporary detaining camps were set up throughout Germany to house the newly freed prisoners, and to make arrangements to send them back to their homelands. Nadia was given information that she would be able to board a transport bound for the U.S.S.R., and she and the Gulker family had immediately prepared for her departure.

There were tears from the girls and hugs from the men. Anton Barton had already left for his home in Poland, and for the second time the Gulkers said goodbye to a faithful worker. Mama Gulker gave her much advice and shed tears herself as she bade farewell to the young

Ukrainian girl who had lived and worked with them for two years.

Johann and Nadia had set out for Hamburg, a day's ride by wagon from Hardinghausen, and there Nadia expected to join the group of men and women who were returning to the Soviet Union. The farewells at the Gulker farm had been difficult for Nadia and she was truly glad that it was Johann who took her to the detaining camp. The two young people talked easily about Nadia's time in Germany. As the wagon rolled along toward Hamburg, Johann tried to reassure Nadia that she would find her relatives alive and well in Soldativ, although secretly he wondered if this would be so. Nadia had received no mail from her family in over a year. The last letter from her sister Maria in Soldativ had indicated that the whole region was under heavy bombing night and day from German planes.

"I will always be grateful to you and your family, Johann, for the kindness you gave to me. I was so frightened when I arrived. I didn't know what to expect," confessed Nadia as the wagon bumped along.

"I know," replied Johann, with a chuckle. "I still remember how you looked by the barn door that day. You resembled a scared rabbit!" The young man turned to look at Nadia. "I am glad you came to trust us, Nadia. It was a difficult situation for all of us. I feel relieved that you leave with good feelings for the Gulker family. We will all miss you, Nadia."

Tears were forming in the eyes of the young woman, and she was glad to see the camp in Hamburg just ahead. For the moment, the two young people turned their attention to their destination, which helped Nadia gain her composure.

Johann drew the wagon up beside the headquarters of the camp and secured the horses at the fence post.

"Wait here, Nadia. I will inquire about the arrangements I must make for you to leave." With that, Johann walked off to find the officer in charge of the camp, with Nadia's identification papers and passport in his hand.

Nadia waited in the wagon on the hard seat for a long time. She began to be more anxious with every passing minute. Finally, Johann returned. Something was wrong! Nadia could see it in his face.

"What is it, Johann? Is there a problem with my papers?" Nadia waited for his reply.

Johann looked at Nadia, finding it hard to meet her steady gaze. "Your papers are in order, Nadia, but the transport to Russia left yesterday. We have missed it by one day. There will be no other ship leaving for some time, maybe months."

Nadia stared at him with unbelieving eyes. "Oh no, Johann! What will I do?"

"I don't know, Nadia," replied the boy, as he climbed back into the wagon. "We must talk about it and decide what is best."

"I'll stay here, Johann, and wait until there is another transport," decided Nadia. After a few minutes of silence Nadia turned to face Johann, who was sitting with his head cradled in his arms.

"That would not be wise. It may be a year before another ship going to Russia is available. No," decided Johann, "you must go back to Hardinghausen with me. Mama will know what to do. You cannot stay here. Anything could happen to you in this kind of a camp."

Against the protest of Nadia, Johann had turned the wagon around and started back toward Hardinghausen, and back to an unknown future for Nadia Chaplya.

Nadia smiled to herself as she savored the coolness of the forest. She remembered the look on the face of Geesken Gulker when she saw Nadia sitting by Johann in the wagon as he returned from

Hamburg. It was late evening when they arrived back at the farm. The household was just beginning to retire. Mama Gulker could not believe what she saw!

"What a shock it was for her," remembered Nadia. "I was afraid she would not know what to do with me."

Geesken Gulker knew what to do. She told Johann that he had done the right thing in bringing Nadia back. It would have been wrong to leave her at that camp, not knowing what might happen to her. Nadia would stay with them until other arrangements could be made for her to return to the Ukraine if she wished. She was welcome to remain and work as before, but not as a prisoner. She was free to decide her own future.

Remembering the words "free to decide the future" caused a frown to crease the lines of Nadia's young face.

"Where is my future?" wondered Nadia. "My mother, if she is alive, must expect that I will return. I don't even know if they survived. But now it is too dangerous to go back! I'll be shot on sight."

Nadia had found out about the conditions in the Ukraine by listening to the reports coming out of the region on short-wave radio. Post-war conditions were very unsettled and it was hard to believe any report that they heard. However, the radio commentators were saying that the Communists had reclaimed authority in the Ukraine and had convinced the villagers that the young people who were taken into Germany as work prisoners in 1943 had really defected and gone willingly into enemy territory to earn money and help the enemy. They should be treated as traitors. The Ukrainian people knew that it was not true, but they were afraid to go against the Communists!

And, of course, there was Joseph! Joseph, who wanted to marry Nadia and take her to England with him to live and set up a tailoring shop. Joseph, who offered Nadia security and his affection, and a new beginning for them both in a different country.

Joseph Kashuba was in Germany as a working prisoner like Maria. He had been released from the farm on which he worked during the course of the war. This tall, dark, nice-looking young man was anxious to begin living again, start building a business and have a family. He had just started helping his father in the Ukraine with a tailoring business when the decree came that sent him off from his homeland as a German prisoner of war. Now, he wanted to rebuild his life.

But he too listened to the news reports from the Ukraine, and he too wondered if it were safe to go back to Kiev.

Joseph had finally made a decision. He would not risk living under threats of another dictator in Russia or anywhere else. He had had enough of that here in Germany under Hitler's rule. Joseph wanted to be free. He decided to go to England and start his own tailoring shop. He had the skills. He wanted a new beginning.

One afternoon, Nadia had come to the camp where Joseph was waiting for a transport to England. Nadia had friends in that camp and it was not too far from the Gulker farm to make the trip by bicycle. Nadia had remained with the Gulker family as she pondered her future and did not have to live in the bare accommodations that her friends did at the camp. She was thankful for that. She had met these Ukrainian young people from other work farms during the war. Mama Gulker had given Nadia the freedom to occasionally visit them, giving them all a connection to their homeland. Now, as they waited for transportation to wherever they chose to live, Nadia often came on her afternoons off from the farm work at Gulkers', enjoying the companionship of her young friends.

Nadia and Joseph met one afternoon and from that point they had spent many a pleasant afternoon together. It was not long before Joseph expressed his feelings to Nadia.

"Go with me to England, Nadia. I am a tailor by trade. Together we will be able to open a tailoring shop and have a good life. There is nothing in the Ukraine for either of us. It is too dangerous to return, and there is no opportunity to make a decent living there."

"Joseph, I am not sure that my feelings for you are as strong as yours for me," responded Nadia. "There is so much to consider."

As the weeks went by, Joseph was more insistent that she go with him, and in the end Nadia agreed to an engagement. She gave him her passport. Joseph began the necessary arrangements for the two of them to leave for England.

However, something within Nadia held her back from making a complete commitment to a life as Joseph's wife. He was a very kind man, and Nadia knew she would be well provided for in England. She did care for Joseph, but was it enough to take such a drastic step? She would have to give up all ideas of seeing her family in Soldativ. What would her mother, if still alive, have to say? Nadia was turning her back on her homeland. Would she be able to discover the fate of her father as well? What had happened to him? After all, Anton Chaplya was still her father, no matter what the circumstances were that had severed that relationship.

But what really bothered her most was the thought of giving up the new source of faith that had come to her in Germany. She went to Mama Gulker to ask for her help.

"Nadia, have you asked the Lord what He would have you do?" asked Mrs. Gulker.

Nadia shook her head. "No, I do not know the Lord in that way. I am only beginning to know about God from the books I read and from hearing the family talk. I have memorized some of the long prayers that are written in your hymn-books but I cannot pray for myself."

Nadia had begun going to church with the Gulkers in Uelsen at the Old German Reformed Church. During the war she was not allowed to attend the services, but now she was welcome to go with the family. Mama Gulker had encouraged Nadia to attend some church of her choosing while she stayed in Germany. Nadia longed to pray, but she did not feel that she had the right to pray. For so long she had turned her back on God, had no place for Him in her life, and even doubted His existence. As she read the books that Mama gave her, she had felt the old bitterness falling away. Nadia didn't understand it, but she felt it. There was a compulsion to know more about God; but to pray? No, Nadia could not.

Nadia made the decision. She would leave Germany with Joseph. There were only two weeks until they would depart. Nadia had begun packing her few possessions, but she was not at peace with the decision. Joseph did not share this new faith that Nadia had begun to know. In England there would be no way that she could continue to learn and be supported in her desire to know God. What was the answer? She cared deeply for Joseph, but was it right to turn her back on God again? Why was she so uneasy?

The nights were long for Nadia. She could not sleep, but lay awake wrestling with the problem.

Finally, late one night, exhausted by the lack of sleep and worry, Nadia knelt by her bed and poured out her heart to the Lord.

"Lord, I am not worthy to ask anything

of You, but help me, I pray. Tell me if I should go to England or stay here. I am lost and need Your guidance."

Her prayer was simple but sincere. God had claimed His child. Nadia had come to Him on her knees, placing her life in His hands.

By morning, Nadia knew that she should not go to England. She felt in her heart that there was something important that she must do in Germany and that God was telling her not to go to England with Joseph. What about the passport? She had given it to Joseph. Nadia knew that there was very little chance that she would get her papers back; however, she would go and try to retrieve them. Nadia borrowed a bike from one of the Gulker girls and set off for the camp to find Joseph.

It was hard to explain her decision to Joseph. Nadia told him all of it. His disappointment was obvious, but he did go with her to the authorities to see if he could regain her passport. Miraculously, they handed it over to Nadia without hesitation. Joseph and Nadia said their farewells, with a few sobs from Nadia. It was hard for Joseph to let Nadia go and it was hard for Nadia to hurt Joseph by refusing to be his wife. Still, the conviction that she was doing the right thing never left her. As difficult as it was, she was sure she was on the right path.

Mama Gulker was watching for Nadia to return. As soon as she saw the girl, she called to her to come and tell her all that had transpired.

"Nadia, what have you done? You left without a word to anyone, child." Geesken Gulker was not scolding Nadia, only expressing concern. "Were you at the camp to see Joseph? Has anything changed?"

"Yes, Mama, I will not be going to England. Last night I finally was able to pray for myself and talked to the Lord. I asked for direction and this morning I was sure what course to take. He heard my prayer, Mama Gulker, and gave me the right words to say to Joseph. I have my passport, too. The authorities gave it to me without a word."

"Nadia, you must continue to pray for the Lord to guide you. You have begun a new life today, one that the Lord God had ready for you. All that was needed was admitting that you could not do this yourself and needed God. I am sure He will lead you now. But, Nadia, you must go and tell all of this to our pastor, Rev. Lankamp. He will know what your next step should be."

•   •   •

Nadia got up from the log and, brushing away the fallen leaves from her skirt, began to call the cows to return to the barn. They knew her voice well, and responded in their slow, plodding manner. As she picked up her book from beside the log where she had sat, the title "Catechism" reminded her that Pastor Lankamp was due to come to the Gulker house tonight. Nadia had taken Mama Gulker's advice and had enjoyed many long conversations with the minister. Nadia smiled as she thought of those talks, of the kindness of Pastor Lankamp. How pleased he was when Nadia told him what had occurred.

"Nadia, God has something important for you to do. He has revealed Himself to you in very unlikely circumstances in a strange land under difficult conditions for you. The Lord has used the Gulker family as His messengers and you must respond by studying, learning, and preparing yourself to be a member of His kingdom. You must study the catechism and become a professing member of His church. That is the first step for you. He will show you the right direction for your life."

Pastor Lankamp had been right. Nadia began to study the materials that he gave her, and with his help she was learning about the love and care of a personal God and, most of all, experiencing that love for herself. The dark and foreboding side of Nadia Chaplya had begun to fade away. God was replacing her anger and resentment with His love. Nadia was crossing over into the light of God.

In two weeks, Nadia would be standing in front of the congregation of the Old German Reformed Church with other young people to declare her faith publicly and become a full member of the church. Nadia was sure that it would be a day she would never forget.

Tonight, Pastor Lankamp was coming to discuss with Nadia and the Gulker family the possibility of finding a sponsor for her to emigrate to the United States. As she entered the rear door of the barn with the cows following behind her, Nadia felt apprehensive about the idea of going so far from her homeland. Was this really something that the Lord wanted her to do? If she did go, she would be giving up all chances of seeing her family in Soldativ again. Would she ever be able to get back again? It was a hard decision, one that Nadia was grateful that she did not have to make alone. She was confident that God would direct her life from this point.

6

A NEW BEGINNING

THE ship tossed up and down in the stormy sea, cutting through the water like an impatient seal. Nadia clung to her berth and wondered if she would survive. She was sick, terribly sick from the constant motion of the waves and wind against the transport. There were forty-two women and children in her cabin, and all of them were experiencing the nausea and diarrhea that assailed Nadia. The two portholes in the cabin were certainly inadequate to provide fresh air for the sour-smelling quarters. To make matters worse, the travelers were all scared, scared of the future and the strange land to which they were headed. They were displaced persons of many different cultures and languages, without a home. All of them had been through the terrors of war and were seeking a land that would offer them peace, a job, and security.

For Nadia, the future was very unsure and she, too, was afraid of what she would find in America. Leaving the Gulkers' home was very hard for her, but they all knew it was time for Nadia to go. Pastor Lankamp had contacted a family in Hamilton, Michigan, in the United States. They would be her sponsors. Nadia would live with them and work for them until she could establish herself.

The entire Gulker family took Nadia to Bremerhaven to board the ship bound for the United States. They had enjoyed their travels together for two weeks before Nadia once more had to say farewell.

"God go with you, Nadia. You will never be alone again. Trust Him to care for you." These were Mama Gulker's parting words to a scared young woman who was now sailing off to the unknown.

Nadia lay in her bunk, trying to find some source of comfort for her aching body. The tossing of the ship had become violent as the weather worsened on the high seas. It would take ten days to cross the Atlantic and reach Boston in the United States, but hopefully not all ten days would be this bad. They were in a converted troopship, one that had ferried men across the ocean to battlefields. Nadia could only feel sorry for men who were carried to war in this manner. It was bad enough to fight, but to be this sick and fight too must have been horrible.

This was not the first time that this

young Ukrainian woman had left the safety of a home. Memories of the day she was taken from her own mother by the Nazi soldiers were still fresh in her mind. That had been six years ago, but the hurt was still there.

"I wonder if my mother survived the war in the Ukraine," mused Nadia as she tried to ignore the pitching of the ship. Lying in her bunk, she could see her mother's face, a mother who always cared for her and worked endless hours to provide for her and the other children. "What about Maria and Boris? Are they still there to care for Mama if she needs help?"

Tears welled up in the young woman's eyes as she realized again that leaving for the United States meant that she would never have answers to these questions. She was sure that she would not be able to look again at that face that had cared for her for eighteen years.

"Mother! How she struggled just to keep us alive!" remembered Nadia.

The journey was different this time for Nadia Chaplya. Before, she had been a lonely prisoner, bitter and resentful toward all the evil around her and the brutal people who had separated her from her loved ones. Her world had been filled with dark, foreboding shadows of uncertainty. But not this time. Nadia was not alone. The God who had meant nothing to her for so long, now had her life in His hand. Her main thought was to somehow do something to thank the Lord for revealing Himself and His love to her in Germany and for lifting the oppressive darkness from her life. He had given her eternal life through Jesus Christ and Nadia was determined to give back to the Lord as much of herself as she could. She didn't know how or where this would happen, but she resolved to live a life of gratitude to God. No, she was not alone on this trip. She felt the Lord's presence every minute she breathed the new life He had given her. She was a full member of His church now, a security that gave her peace of mind and heart as never before.

Crossing the Atlantic Ocean was an experience that Nadia decided she would not repeat if she had a choice. The ten days were endless and uncomfortable. As she stood on the deck of the ship which was quietly gliding through the water on this cloudless summer day, she saw the harbor of Boston come into view with a tremendous sense of relief. But, now what? She spoke no English. There would be many difficulties to overcome.

"You don't seem very happy to be here,

Nadia. Are you frightened?" The voice belonged to a young man from the Ukraine whom she had met on board the ship.

"Yes, I'm afraid, but I've been through this before. A strange country, a new language, living with people I don't know, it's all too familiar," replied Nadia.

"I know how you feel. It's not comforting to be alone," replied the tall youth. Brushing back his dark hair that had become rather unruly from the neglect of the long sea voyage, he looked at Nadia and said, "Perhaps we can correspond, Nadia?"

"No, I don't think so," responded the slender girl standing beside him, looking at the United States for the first time. "That might not please the family that will provide for me. I must be careful not to offend them in any way. But you are wrong about me being alone, Vladimir. The Lord Jesus Christ is always with me. It is a great comfort to me to know that He will direct the events of my life. I wish for you the same comfort."

Everyone began to collect their belongings and disembark onto the busy pier at Boston Harbor. The process of entering the United States was difficult, long and exhausting—the beginning of endless lines, stacks of forms to fill out, and confusing directions to try to follow.

Finally, Nadia was finished with the tedious processing and she sat nervously awaiting the arrival of the train that would take her to Kalamazoo, Michigan. The young woman had all of her belongings in one small suitcase and a note pinned to her coat that said "No English." She was beginning to feel very weary.

Nadia was hungry. She watched people go into the shop to buy sandwiches, but she was afraid to move from the spot that had been assigned to her. She had a small amount of money in her pocket but she could not bring herself to go into the shop, so she sat and nibbled on the piece of old bread that she had kept from her lunch the day before and tried not to think about the food that others ate around her.

She was put on the train for Kalamazoo by the official in charge of a group of departing immigrants. The conductor was informed that she spoke no English. Nadia leaned back against the rough upholstery of the seat of the railroad car and, suddenly, unpleasant thoughts came to her as she remembered another railroad trip six years before in the Ukraine. There had been armed guards at the door and frightened young people on their way to Germany standing in the cattle car. Nadia turned to the window to look at the passing scenery of this new country and thanked God for His goodness to her. The panic from remembering the terror of Soldativ and Kiev passed. Her heart was full of gratitude for being a child of God, chosen by Him to receive redemption.

John Nyboer and his wife met her at the station. They were friends of Pastor Lankamp in Germany and had consented to be Nadia's sponsors. Nadia tightly gripped her wooden suitcase, feeling uncertainty anew. All of her possessions were in that small case marked "Nadija Tschaplya,* Hamilton, Mich., USA." She had no money, no family, just one suitcase packed with a few clothes and books and her Bible. She reminded herself that she was here to serve her God in any way He wanted, as she looked at the two strange people waiting for her. The situation was very awkward at first, but with the first greetings over they headed for Nadia's new home in Hamilton, Michigan.

Hamilton is in the heart of the agricultural center of Michigan. The lush green countryside is abundant with celery farms. Black, rich soil makes a sharp and beautiful contrast to the bright green of growing, healthy plants. These people of

---

* The German spelling of her name.

Hamilton were all of Dutch heritage, very proud, very industrious, and very dedicated to their religious beliefs. Most of the activities in the small community revolved around farm and church activities.

The Nyboer farm in Hamilton was modest in size but always teaming with activity, with many chores to be done everyday. Nadia remembered the farm life in Germany with the Gulker family and longed for the warmth of those dear people. But this was a new land and a new family, and Nadia put forth the same energy into her daily routine as before. It was not unusual to see this young, dark-haired Ukrainian girl sitting high atop Mr. Nyboer's big tractor doing a lion's share of the work.

Nadia stayed with the Nyboers for six weeks. An opportunity to work in a sewing factory became available to her so Nadia made another move. This time to nearby Graafschap to live with the Diekjacobs family. She worked hard, did her task well, but something seemed to be missing.

Nadia was restless. She felt that she was not doing enough to show her gratitude to her Lord. Farm work and factory work were both good, respectable jobs, but deep within she sensed that God was saying "Move on, Nadia. There is more for you to do in My name."

Finally, she made the decision to work at the Pine Rest Christian Mental Health Services in Grand Rapids, Michigan, a very large nursing and counseling facility operated by the Christian Reformed Church. Her job was in food service and kitchen work, but she could feel the excitement of being surrounded by Christian people busily working to help others, whether it was in the nursing department, the administration section, or in the kitchen area. Everyone had the same goal: serve the Lord by helping to ease the pain and distress of others, in Christ's name.

Nadia studied English as well as nursing in her off-hours at Pine Rest Hospital. She wanted more education, more opportunity to advance in a career, but she found opposition in an unexpected detail.

Nadia had applied to take the courses offered at Pine Rest to become a certified nurse of psychiatry. Her application was granted. But Nadia was stunned to hear that she could not go to work on the floor with patients while she interned.

"I don't understand. Why do you feel this way?"

Nadia had asked the question, but she was not really sure she wanted an answer. The old feeling of not being worthy surfaced again, and here she was once more battling rejection from a very unexpected quarter. But that was not really true. The administrator only thought that it would be hard for the patients to understand Nadia's words, still heavy with the Ukrainian accent. Nadia had momentarily slipped back into the old habit of viewing herself as worthless. She realized that she needed the direction of the Lord.

"Lord, You have taught me that I am not worthless, but have value as Your child. If it be Your will, I want to study to be a nurse. I want to show my gratitude to You for Your goodness to me and be well equipped to share Your gospel with others."

Confident in her prayer, Nadia continued to work hard, not unlike Oksana of her childhood. Nadia had learned well from her mother to see to the needs of others first, then take care of Nadia Chaplya.

Nadia Chaplya. Her name was proving difficult for those around her to pronounce. No one could spell it or say it without asking, "What kind of a name is that?"

"Choose a new name, Nadia," suggested a friend. "When you become a citizen of

the United States, start a new chapter in
your life with a new name."

And thus Nadia Chaplya became 'Nancy
Chapel,' and a citizen of the United States.
It was close to her real name, close
enough that Nadia did not feel as if she
had totally abandoned her Ukrainian
identity.

Nancy was admitted to the nursing program two months later and earned her
certificate. Her prayer was answered. She
worked in the hospital at Pine Rest for
several years, gaining valuable experience
in dealing with people in distress, men-
tally ill for various reasons. No one could
have been better equipped to deal with
the distress of others than the dark-
haired young woman from the Ukraine
who had experienced all of the evil and
distress that man could devise.

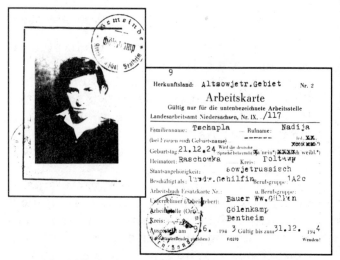

Identification papers and work permits.

*Nadia's wooden suitcase with her name
(as spelled in German) carved into it.*

7

ALL THAT IS POSSIBLE

THE way that God had shaped the per-
sonality of this young woman from the
Ukraine was a wonder to behold! Through
all of the horrors of poverty, famine, persecution and war, Nancy Chapel would be
the first to say that nothing good could
possibly come of all the evil she had experienced.

But, God was carefully molding and re-
fining the life and character of Nancy to
be His ambassador and servant. In
Soldativ and Rashevka she had learned
how to survive, how to have little and
make it adequate. She gained a work ethic
from her mother in the Ukraine that enabled her to endure servitude in Germany
and ultimately earn the respect and love
of her enemies there.

Nadia became strong, determined, capable of handling any task set before her,
and with these things in place, the Lord
put the key piece into the picture to make
it whole. He revealed His love and promises to Nancy. Now, ten years later, Nancy
could see His leading and recognized the

reason for all the suffering that she endured. She could only feel very humble in reflection and was committed to complete the picture by devoting her life to His service, placing that life in His hand.

To serve God was the compelling force behind Nancy's desire to be completely educated and equipped to teach others about God and His redemptive gospel. She decided to leave Pine Rest after three years and enroll at Reformed Bible Institute in Grand Rapids, Michigan, to take courses that would enable her to become a Bible teacher in the Bible Women program offered by the CRC World Missions Board. Nancy would be able to go to the mission field without a full four-year teaching certificate and could work with women of the mission area, teaching Bible and Home Economics. It meant hard work again, more part-time jobs to pay tuition and living expenses, but Nancy was no stranger to hard work.

Nancy needed a new church home, one that was nearer to RBI. The school officials suggested Mayfair Christian Reformed Church, which was within walking distance of the school's campus. Little did she know at the time that she joined that congregation what a major role these people would play in her life.

Sid and Mary Hoogeboom were members of Mayfair, both very active in the missions program of the church. On this particular Saturday afternoon, Mary was busy in the kitchen at home, getting things ready for Sunday. The telephone rang in the family room and Mary called to her husband, "Would you get that, Sid. My hands are full."

"Sure," was the answer from the hallway. Mary continued to chop the fruit for the pie and gave no more thought to the ringing phone.

"That was Rev. Verhulst calling," reported Sid, coming into the kitchen and reaching for a piece of the apple being sliced. "There is a young woman from the Ukraine attending RBI, who has joined our church. He thinks she needs a friend to keep tabs on her progress and thought maybe we could do that."

"You must mean Nancy Chapel," stated Mary, who was always well informed concerning new members at Mayfair. "Give me her number, Sid, and I'll invite her for Sunday dinner."

That was the beginning of a long friendship for Nancy and a cherished relationship for the three of them.

At last Nancy was studying to teach. She would be qualified to be a part of a program that witnessed to those who did not know the Lord Jesus Christ. Nancy knew what it was like to be without God. She could testify from personal experience to the difference in her life with the Lord as the focal point of all she did.

The classrooms of Gadyach in the Ukraine were a part of the past for Nadia, but she still could remember the excitement of study and the joy of learning. Here in Grand Rapids, Michigan, in a Christian institute, the same thrill surrounded her. This time the work was for the Lord to be used as He willed, not for Nadia Chaplya to advance herself. The love of study was still present in this young woman, but now she had a direction, a purpose, a reason to learn all she could to better serve her Lord.

After two years of study and work, graduation from RBI was near for Nancy. But a complication arose.

"Now what am I to do?" asked a frustrated Nancy. She was sitting at the table in the Hoogebooms' kitchen and facing Mary and Sid.

"What's the problem, Nancy?"

Everything had been progressing quite well as far as Sid could tell and this question puzzled him. "Aren't you going into the Bible Women program, Nancy?"

"That's the problem. They have closed the program. All of this work and now where am I? It's almost as if the Lord is telling me that He doesn't want me to teach in His name!"

"Nancy, you know better than that. This door is closed but the Lord will open the right one for you," replied Sid.

"I applied at the Foreign Mission Board and they tell me I need more education—a degree in teaching—before I will be qualified for their programs. There is an opening to go to the Indian field here in the States, but I am not sure what to do."

Mary looked at Nancy and sensed the unrest in the young woman, as well as the deep disappointment that she could not work with the Bible Women program.

"Another setback for this girl," thought Mary to herself. "She certainly has had her share!" Out loud, she said, "Nancy, enroll at Calvin College here in town and get your teaching degree. You will have done all that is possible then."

Sitting in the office of the registrar a month later, Nancy remembered those words, "all you can possibly do." Nancy had been in this chair in this office once before and had been flatly refused admission to Calvin College.

"You must have documentation of your

high school record, Miss Chapel. We cannot count courses from RBI for credit and we need proof of your academic record," was the answer the administrator had given her.

"How can I get such proof?" responded a puzzled young woman. "They are all in the Ukraine or burned up in the bombings during the war. I have no records left."

"I am sorry, Miss Chapel. But I will have to refuse you admission at this time," was the reply.

Here she was again. One more try. She had her application in her hand and if the Lord wanted her here, only He could open this closed door.

Before she came this morning, Nancy went on her knees in personal prayer to God. "If this is the way I should go, Lord, if this is the place where You want me, open a door for me to serve You. Let me know Your will."

"Good morning, Miss Chapel" was the greeting from the registrar as he hurriedly entered the office and sat behind his desk. "So good to see you. We have been reviewing your case carefully after you called for this appointment again, and I think we can work things out for you to enroll in the fall classes this year. Does that meet with your approval?"

The words startled Nancy. She was speechless. The Lord had answered her prayers. Nothing else could possibly have changed the situation so dramatically.

"Yes, yes, of course I am pleased," replied Nancy. "I will also need part-time jobs to help me with the tuition and living."

"We will be glad to give you any assistance you might need, Miss Chapel. Fill out the necessary forms this afternoon and we will set things in motion for you to begin your classes in September."

Nancy left the office with her head in a whirl, still having a hard time fully believing what she had just heard, but praising God for His goodness to her!

"Letters for you, Miss Chapel," chirped the postman who delivered her mail each day. He was at her apartment house mailboxes as Nancy returned to her apartment. "Nice day, eh?"

"Yes, yes, it *is* a nice day! Praise God for it," replied Nancy.

Nancy took the mail and opened the door to her apartment, slowly going through the letters at the same time. There was one envelope with an unfamiliar return address on it. Nancy opened the letter. She had to sit down. Her knees would not hold her. She was looking at a check made out to Calvin College for her tuition for the first semester of study at the college. The check was from Sid Hoogeboom's sister. Nancy gave thanks to the Lord for turning the impossible into opportunity.

All of the trials that Nancy had endured in her life, as terrifying as they were, helped her succeed in this new challenge. She knew how to work hard. She knew how to stay with a task until it was done. Oksana had taught her that! Nancy also knew the source of help when human spirits failed—the Lord and His never failing strength.

With hard work and many part-time jobs, Nancy graduated from Calvin with a BA degree and a Secondary Teaching Certificate in three years instead of the usual four. She didn't take a summer vacation. She continued through the year, never having a break or time away from study or work. No time to stop, relax and enjoy life around her. She was totally focused and determined to earn her degree as soon as possible. At last she felt that she was equipped to teach and share the gospel wheresoever God wanted her to go. The picture was complete.

The last piece of the Lord's design was

put into place.

"How do you feel, Nancy?" inquired Mary, as they both looked at the leather-bound diploma in Nancy's hand.

"Very humble and unworthy that the Lord has gone to such lengths to make me His child. I am just ordinary, nothing special, and to think that He brought me to this point all the way from the darkness of the Ukraine. What an Almighty God we have!"

8

IN GOD'S SERVICE

"HI, Nancy!" The sandy-haired, slender man came briskly over to where she was sitting near the airstrip. "I'm Ray Browneye and everything is ready for us to leave if you are."

Ray was the mission pilot for the Christian Reformed Board of World Missions, headquartered in Grand Rapids, Michigan. Nancy had heard about this energetic young man and his wife, Ann, who served as missionaries in Nigeria.

In his Cessna 414, Ray had made many a dangerous trip over this rough terrain in all kinds of weather, to take missionaries to their remote posts or to give a helping hand to get medical attention to the people in the bush of Africa quickly.

With this short introduction to Ray, Nancy replied, "I'm ready, Ray." When all of her gear was stowed on board the plane, Ray taxied to the end of the runway. There he stopped and turned to look at Nancy. "A wonderful day to fly, Nancy. Let's ask the Lord's blessing on our flight."

With that said, Ray offered a prayer to

God for His protection as they traveled and gave thanks to Him for His goodness in bringing Nancy to work in Nigeria.

Nancy was soon to learn that this mission pilot never let the wheels of his plane leave the runway without a prayer for God's guidance.

Once they were airborne, Nancy looked down over the terrain below. It was rugged but beautiful, lush green with great mountains looming in the far-distant east. Great billowing white clouds floated through the calm blue sky.

"This is a long way from the Ukraine, Ray. I will need many prayers to do this task."

"Oh, you'll do just fine, Nancy. The Mission Board knows a good missionary when they see one," chuckled Ray. Ray had become a master in the art of relaxing his passengers, some of whom were terrified speechless of flying, even to the point of holding on tightly to him. Difficult to fly a plane that way!

"You'll have to study the language first, but from what we hear, you are rather good at learning languages." Again, that ready smile appeared on Ray Browneye's face as he tried to reassure Nancy.

As the plane soared through the sky, Nancy could only marvel at the events that had finally brought her to this point. Now, she could really begin to do something tangible to thank God for His goodness to her.

After graduation from Calvin, the Board of Foreign Missions offered her a job teaching young girls in Uavande, Nigeria. This was not what Nancy had in mind, but she went to the Lord in prayer and asked for His direction. God finally convinced her that this was where He wanted her to serve Him. So, she went to Nigeria.

Another foreign country, another language to learn, more frightening situations ahead for this young Ukrainian woman to confront, but this time it was the Lord's task and His choosing. He would provide all she needed to do the work.

"The work may be hard at first, Nancy, but slowly you will become acclimated to the different climate and customs. We have a great support system here: God and each other!" declared Ray, settling down for a pleasant flight.

Before Nancy arrived in Nigeria, she had stopped in Germany for three weeks to visit the Gulker family in Hardinghausen. The family met her at the docks in Rotterdam, Holland, to welcome her back into their midst after ten years. There was one member of the family who did not make the journey. Mama Gulker was bedridden after a severe stroke.

The Gulker family had expanded in ten years. Five of the children were married and some had children of their own. It was a great reunion and a wonderful three weeks. Memories came flooding back to Nancy as she remembered the days of hard work on the Gulker farm, the smiles of the twins, Hanni and Frieda, and the blessed family that was instrumental in bringing her to a point where she was receptive to the will of the Lord Jesus Christ.

"How different my life has been since that time," thought Nancy. "The peace and security in my heart is unbelievable. My anger and resentment melted away under God's love. He made me complete and whole, not just a shell of a person with no love and no purpose. Praise God for this new life of mine!"

Nancy smiled to herself as she silently reviewed all of the faces of the family and tried to remember the new ones. She was saddened by the condition of Mama Gulker, but the two of them had been able to have good conversations while she was at the Gulker home.

"How was your trip across from the

U.S., Nancy?" inquired Ray, breaking into Nancy's train of thought. "Did you have smooth sailing?"

"I told myself that I would never take another ship across the Atlantic again after I went across to the United States the first time on a troop carrier. This time I really mean it; I will not travel that way again. It just doesn't agree with me."

The mission field in Nigeria to which Nancy was going had been started in 1911 by Dutch missionaries connected with the Dutch Reformed Church. The harvest was slow in the beginning and it was almost twenty-five years before there were apparent fruits of their labors. But the labor continued on, bringing the gospel to the Tiv people in Nigeria, even though converts were few. Still, the seeds were being sown and the missionaries trusted God to give the increase.

It became financially difficult for the Dutch Reformed Church to continue supporting the various mission fields in Nigeria, and the officials of the DRCN (Dutch Reformed Church of Nigeria) approached the Christian Reformed Foreign Mission Board in the United States to consider taking over the work in that part of Africa. So in 1919 they formally took over the work from the Dutch Reformed Church.

to Nigeria

Now, in 1959, Nancy was coming to teach at the Uavande Primary School for Girls which was now under the direction of Miss Geraldine VandenBerg, principal. The girls at this school were taught all of the academic subjects as well as domestic skills such as cooking and sewing. It was a boarding school, so Nancy would be responsible for these girls day and night. It seemed like an overwhelming task. But, as Ray had said, there was a great support team in place. Nancy would cherish the help of her fellow missionaries and God!

Nancy thought about these young Nigerian girls. Would she be able to present the gospel to them so that it was meaningful? Would she be able to show them the difference it makes in your life to have the love of the Lord in your heart? Could she help to bring them into the light of Jesus Christ?

"One thing I will surely tell them," decided Nancy, "is that if God would bother to snatch an unbelieving Ukrainian girl out of the darkness of Russia and claim her for His own, He will certainly do the same in the heart of a Nigerian. I can share with them the fact that the Lord brought love to me instead of hate. He made my heart available for His gospel and gave me the greatest gift of all, salvation in Jesus Christ. The Lord has that same love ready for these girls in Nigeria." Nancy remembered where she had first heard the words "God has His love ready for you." Mama Gulker had told her thirteen years ago in Germany that God had His love ready for her. All she needed was to admit that she needed God and needed His love.

Nancy looked out over the African land below the plane and she felt tremendous thankfulness that the Lord was a God for Ukrainians, Germans, Americans, as well as Nigerians, and indeed, the entire world.

Ray was busy talking to the control tower in Gboko, their destination today. Zaki Biam had no landing strips, so the rest of the trip would be made by car. There was always someone willing to drive you in his car to your destination or lend you a moped or a bike for your journey. More of their "support system," as Ray had said.

Nancy thought about another support system, hers exclusively. It was the congregation of Mayfair Christian Reformed Church back in Grand Rapids, Michigan.

"My 'love family,'" thought Nancy. "They are the closest thing to my real family as possible. And those dear children of the

Sunday School! They were so enthusiastic. I will miss all of them."

Months before, as Nancy was preparing to leave for Nigeria, her church was determined to have a part in her mission work. The Sunday School children of Mayfair made Nancy their special project. All of their collections went to Nancy to help in Nigeria. The ladies of the church had a shower for Nancy to help her gather together the necessary household goods for her house in Nigeria. The congregation had decided to sponsor Nancy as their missionary and help with her financial needs. Nancy was overwhelmed by their display of love and concern. Over and over, she was assured that they would be praying for her regularly and would correspond often. Nancy was "their missionary," and they wanted to help in any way possible. And now, she was here. Here in Nigeria, where at last she could work in God's kingdom and share her love and the gospel of her Lord and Savior. Now she could begin to give thanks to the Lord in a tangible way for His snatching her out of darkness. She would do all she could to bring the gospel to His children in Nigeria for His glory alone.

Laura Beelen stood in the doorway of her house in Zaki Biam. With outstretched arms she welcomed Nancy to Nigeria and her home.

"I have been looking forward to having you, Nancy. If you like, you may stay with me for the four months of language study here," offered the woman. "If I can help you, I will be delighted to do so."

Nancy did stay with Laura for the required four months. The course was difficult, as Nancy was required to learn the Tiv language. She would be teaching in English and the local Tiv dialect. However, Nancy had a natural flair for languages that enabled her to learn easily. She was not inhibited by the fear of "sounding strange" as she attempted to converse in Tiv. Nancy had conquered that barrier a long time ago in Germany. This would be the fourth language in which she was able to converse and write fluently. Quite an accomplishment for a thirty-five-year-old woman!

Now, four months later, the house that Nancy was standing in front of was *her* house. The time had gone by quickly in Zaki Biam, and before long it was time to be off to Uavande. The ride had been bumpy on the deeply rutted, narrow road, and she was covered with dust that blew from the Sahara Desert. The constant breeze called "harmattan" left a layer of beige dust on everything this time of year.

It was a well-built house of brick, wash-ed white with a cement coating. There was no electricity or indoor plumbing.

For some people this would have been a hard adjustment to make, but Nancy had grown up without these conveniences. She knew how to live this way.

The kitchens in the houses of Nigeria were traditionally kept separate from the living quarters. Sometimes they were in a different building behind the home.

Iwar had begun unloading the many suitcases and boxes. Nancy looked at the young Nigerian and hoped that they could work well together. For in Zaki Biam one day, as the time of language study was nearing completion, Laura had informed Nancy that they must look for a houseboy to go to Uavande with her.

Nancy was horrified. "Laura, I don't need a houseboy to do my work! I can do it myself! I don't think I should have someone working for me."

"It is the custom here, Nancy, that you have domestic help. It is expected," ex-plained Laura. "Our days are long; some-times we put in twelve hours, and you will be very thankful that someone is there to fix meals and do the housework for you."

Their search had led them to Iwar, who

was now busy carrying boxes into the house. He knew very little about being a housekeeper and cook, however. Nancy would have to teach him many things. But he had been willing to go to Uavande to be Nancy's houseboy.

Nancy soon learned just how much she had to teach Iwar about cooking. The first breakfast that he cooked for her was fried pickles! From that low point, Nancy could only expect improvement!

Uavande is situated in a valley with great mountains rising in the east, and from the porch of the long, one-story schoolhouse Nancy could see the beauty of this African country. The students were all housed in round huts with thatched roofs, grouped around the compound. The girls of the school had been told that a new teacher would soon arrive, but even though they were prepared for her arrival, there were snickers and shy giggles as Nancy came into the classroom.

"This will be a challenge," thought Nancy. However, Nancy was a hard worker and always well prepared to teach her subjects. She possessed a high level of enthusiasm and was never idle for a moment.

As the girls soon discovered, this dark-haired young woman was also a stern disciplinarian. She expected hard work from her students and she meant to keep order, have work done on time, and keep to a schedule every day.

Slowly, Nancy settled into a routine with her students. She taught them English and increased her knowledge of the Tiv dialect. There were times when things were difficult, times when the girls were trying, times when Nancy wondered how she would cope. Prayer sustained her, gave her strength in the Lord to do His work. She coped with temper tantrums, tears of frustration from her students, and all of the usual problems associated with teenage girls. Quite a challenge!

Through it all, Nancy became close to her students, helping them in difficult times at school away from their homes and families. Often, Nancy would visit the huts of their families, trying to know her students better and building a relationship with the people.

Nancy taught the girls to sew. They made the uniforms that they wore to school, feeling a sense of accomplishment. She taught them to cook and do household jobs. In the classroom Nancy was strict, but she always shared her love with them. They called her "Miss," a simple name that Nancy cherished.

Early one morning, Geraldine Vanden-Berg came looking for Nancy before classes started. "I must talk to you and the other helpers, Nancy. We have a crisis on our hands."

Nancy followed the principal into the school and went about getting the coffee pot ready. As soon as everyone was assembled, Gerry took out a letter from her folder.

"I have a note from the Secretary General in Mkar. He says that there is fighting going on between two of the tribes in this area and he believes it is not safe for us to stay here, so far out in the bush country. He recommends we close up and evacuate to Mkar." Gerry looked at her staff for a minute or two and let the news sink in.

"I have already responded for myself, but you each must decide what to do. I wrote and told him that there is no way that I could send these girls home now. The roads are too dangerous with these bands on the street, and I can't leave them here alone. So, I will stay, but you must each make your own decision."

Without a moment of hesitation, Nancy responded to Gerry's question. "I will also stay. I am not afraid for my life. It is the Lord's to do with as He will, and I am sure that He will protect us here."

The decision was typical of Nancy's strong commitment to the Lord and her strong faith in His guardianship over her life for His purpose. This was the message that the girls at Uavande school received from the teaching and example of Nancy Chapel.

9

THE LORD, MY SHIELD

D ARKNESS engulfed the Uavande school complex in Nigeria. The business of the day was over. Iwar had finished his household chores and had returned to his own house outside the compound. Weary teachers and students enjoyed a refreshing sleep, and the quietness of night seemed to signal that all was well, peaceful and serene. But that was not the case.

Nancy Chapel sat in the cramped pantry of her house near the school compound and tried to control her racing emotions. She was shaking with fright, praying constantly for help. She was locked in—locked in by eight intruders looking for money.

Nancy had gone to bed early that night. She was tired, and ached from her head to her toes. She was trying to cope with a recurring bout of malaria—which usually assailed her at the most inopportune times. Her head was swimming from the four pills that she had taken before retiring, and the last thing that she needed was to be routed out of bed abruptly by eight roving bandits at three o'clock in the morning!

She had heard commotion outside and caught her name being called. "Principal!" a harsh voice shouted. "Where are you?" Bright flashlight beams were searching for her house.

Nancy had become the principal of Uavande School when Gerry VandenBerg was assigned to another station. The person that these intruders were searching for was Nancy.

"I am here," she shouted from her window. "I heard Becky Agbo cry out. What have you done to her?" Becky was one of the Nigerian teachers at the compound. "What is your business here?"

"We want your money, all of it. Give it to us now," was the reply.

Nancy knew that she and Becky were alone in the compound except for the girls who were sleeping nearby in their huts. There was usually a guard at the gate throughout the night, but where was he now? That morning she had collected the fees from the girls for the coming semester and had put that money in the school's safe.

"All that money is in the safe. Someone must have told them that I collected the fees today. I must quickly hide those

keys," decided Nancy, and before she answered the man's call for money, she
slipped the ring of keys under the rug by
the door. Nancy silently prayed, "Lord,
don't let them remember the safe in the
school!"

The intruders were banging on the side
of the house now, impatient to have the
money.

Nancy took her own purse and emptied
it. Not wanting to open a door to these
hoodlums, Nancy pushed the money out
of her window and gave it to one of the
men.

They became enraged. "This is too
small. Where is the rest of your money?"
they shouted.

"That is all that I have. I gave you my
last bill. Now go and leave us in peace."

That was not the plan of these eight
men. Nancy heard the crash of her front
door and was dismayed to see the men
walk into her bedroom. Room by room,
they began to tear everything apart. Eight
men with eight guns! Nancy's bed was
ripped apart and the mattress thrown on
the floor. One of the men began shoving
Nancy around the room. With a gun bar-
rel held to her temple, he demanded that
she give them more money.

"I am not afraid of you. I belong to

Jesus. I am telling you that I have no more money here."

One of the men took Nancy's flashlight from her and shoved her into the pantry, locking the door behind him. From the dark confines of the closet-size room, Nancy could hear them ransacking the house. She sat in total darkness, wondering if Becky was all right and if they would be killed at any minute.

"Lord, please don't let them remember the school safe. Make them forget it," Nancy prayed again.

At that moment, the pantry door was unlocked and pulled open.

"Where are the keys for the suitcases here?" demanded one of the bandits. "Give them to me." Nancy realized that she could not give him those keys. The keys to the suitcases and trunk were on the same ring as the safe key. She was not going to give them the key to the school safe.

"I don't have those keys. I lost them somewhere. Just break off the locks. I don't care about them anyway. Split it open. It's all right."

The men were not prepared for this answer and were puzzled by her willingness to have them break into her luggage. After a bit of grumbling, they decided to shove

Nancy back in the pantry and told her to remain there or else. The "or else," as they described it, was not very pleasant. Then, abruptly, they left. Still without light, Nancy could only sit down on the floor and wait until dawn. She thanked God for sparing her life and for making the men forget about the school safe full of money.

Should she try to look out to see if they were gone? Nancy could not hear any voices. Miraculously the girls were still asleep, undisturbed by the intruders. Cautiously Nancy opened the pantry door and peered out into the dim light of approaching dawn. She saw no one and decided to risk going out to see if Becky was hurt.

Nancy found Becky just coming out of her house, still shaken, but, like Nancy, unwilling to remain indoors any longer.

"Are you all right?" inquired Nancy of the young Tiv woman. "I heard you scream when the men first came into the compound."

"They slapped me a few times, but I am all right. I didn't want to tell them where you were, but in the end I had to tell them. I can't imagine what happened to the gate guard! Did they hurt you?"

"Thanks be to God, they didn't hurt me

or get the money from the safe in the school. I prayed that God would make them forget about that school safe. Those robbers will be very angry when they realize what they missed!" Nancy could feel her knees begin to shake and sat down on the porch of Becky's house.

Throughout the day, the news of the robbery was the topic of conversation in the compound. Nancy's pupils flocked around her as she came into the schoolhouse.

"Oh, Miss, weren't you terribly afraid? Why didn't you just scream?" inquired the girls, who were accustomed to using the "screaming technique" for many purposes.

The girls quickly gathered around Nancy on the school porch, anxious to hear all the details of this scary situation.

"I have taught you about God's grace in your lessons. I have told you that God will answer your prayers and protect you. Now you see the practical application of that truth.

"God was there with me, standing between me and those men. I prayed that the men would not remember the money in the school and He did that too."

Nancy looked at the faces of the girls who were trying hard to absorb the words of their principal.

"What I am trying to tell you is that God's grace is real, not just words in a book, but real. You must have that kind of faith, strong and trusting. Then God will be at your side in every way. He took away my fear and helped me handle the men the right way. He was my shield and I am grateful to Him that His promises are true, real for me and real for you."

Sewing class at Uavande school.

Uavande schoolgirls carry water, wood and knit and sew at the same time.

10

WITH GOD'S LOVE

NIGERIA. Nancy Chapel's home for almost twenty years. The country and
the people became the consuming pas-
sion of the heart and spirit of this Ukrainian woman. Her despairs, the hurts, the
loss of family and home, were all orchestrated by God to give Nancy the compassion of mind and the strength of resolve
to minister to His people in Nigeria.

The people of Tivland were not just bodies to be evangelized and taught, but they
were Nancy's friends, a relationship that
still endures and is nourished by many
letters to and from Nigeria. To relate in a
positive way to those of a different culture
and different temperament is not an easy
task. Only with a great measure of patience, love and understanding is this possible. Nancy Chapel possessed those
qualities. With the Lord's help she was
able to see through the eyes of the Nigerians and appreciate them for the fine
people that they were. She did not at-
tempt to change their customs or attitudes to fit Western standards but

brought the message of God's love to them in their world.

"You know, there is one character flaw that Nigerians pick up instantly," shared Nancy. "They can spot insincerity every time, and often long before we who have come as missionaries recognize it. They know if you are talking as you believe or just talking!"

Nancy taught the Tiv children with her usual Christian zeal. She equipped them with academic skills so they might become a valuable part of their society and be able to make a real contribution to the development and nurture of their culture. Nancy gave them a basis for life, a working, true relationship between them and the Lord Jesus Christ. This did not come to these young people just from the textbooks alone. Nancy was a living, working, vibrant witness of what a child of God should be. The Tiv people saw her in good times and in bad, and in each they felt the strength of commitment and spirit of a Christ-centered woman who loved them dearly as brothers and sisters in the Lord. Nancy was real and her love for the Lord was real, and the people she taught and lived among saw it and embraced her.

After eight years of teaching Tiv young women at Uavande, Nancy was asked in

1968 to go to Harga to teach at the newly established Benue Bible Institute. This school was established to give regular religious instruction to those who would become teachers in the Tiv community. The founders of the Institute felt that it was extremely important for them to know God's Word thoroughly and to understand His teachings completely before they began their various teaching assignments. What was needed was a centralized Tiv Bible training school, and Benue Bible Institute filled that need.

Nancy went from teaching young women to instructing entire families. At BBI, married Bible students brought their families with them, and this presented the teachers with an avenue to influence their lives in every area. Nancy made a significant contribution at Harga, again drawing from her personal life and experiences.

In 1971, the Nigerian Christian Church (NKST), with the help of the established mission field of the CRC and the government, opened a Girl's Secondary School at Uavande. Nancy Chapel served as principal of that school until 1973. A year later, she moved to Zaki Biam to be first a teacher and then principal of the secondary co-educational schools.

Nancy's last assignment in Nigeria in

1976 was in Mkar, at the Teacher's College in that town. One of the commitments of the CRC church in Nigeria was to teach the young men and women academic subjects as well as give Bible instruction, so that they might eventually assume the leadership role in their country and so that the missionaries would be able to turn the instruction of their young people over to well-qualified Nigerian teachers.

This teaching assignment included both men and women. Nancy taught academic courses as well as courses in religious knowledge, and both Christian and Muslim history. But Nancy wanted them to have more. It was here at Mkar that Nancy spent countless hours outlining the entire Old Testament, complete with questions and answers on each chapter. A major task! Her outline was an invaluable contribution to the Bible study program in Mkar. Every Sunday afternoon she held a Bible study for those who wanted to come and learn more about the God that this Ukrainian woman served and loved.

Nancy had filled the life of so many Nigerians with the knowledge of Jesus Christ. She gave them the understanding of what living as a Christian believer was all about. But, for Nancy, there was a part of her personal life that had been left in-complete.

"Nancy," inquired Fran Bratt, a nurse from Grand Rapids who had come to Mkar Medical Facility with her husband, Dr. Harvey Bratt, to volunteer their time at the hospital there, "what about your family in the Ukraine?"

This was the question that was always just below the surface in the mind of Nancy Chapel, but never quite addressed. In quiet moments Nancy's thoughts often drifted back to her family in the Ukraine. Did they survive the war? Did her father return to Soldativ or die as a political prisoner in the depths of Siberia? And what about her sister Maria and her brother Boris? Did they care for her mother? All questions with no answers, only speculations that frightened Nancy. It was better to keep busy and not think so much!

"Fran, I just don't dare try to find them if they are still alive. The Communists who rule there can be very cruel. If they find out that my family has a relative living outside Russia who is prospering, it might bring more persecution to them. I'm sure they have suffered enough. Maybe they are alive and I could correspond with them, but the authorities would find out. Mail is opened as a routine procedure in the U.S.S.R. Nothing is personal or private. Going there myself is out of the question," pointed out Nancy. "You forget I am still a traitor to the government in the Ukraine. That will not change."

"Someday, Nancy, I hope it will change and you can put that issue to rest. Meantime, we are your family, all of us. You are very dear to your colleagues, your church members and friends in Grand Rapids, and certainly to the Bratt family," declared Fran. Actually, all of the Bratt children who were now studying at Hillcrest School in Jos called Nancy "Aunt Nancy."

Nancy enjoyed a close relationship with many people. Mail delivery in Mkar was sure to produce an abundance of letters for Nancy from many parts of the world. Her "adopted sister" Jenny Sytsma, in Holland, Michigan, wrote letters every week. Nancy had lived for a while with Jenny's family there and the two young women had become very close friends.

There was also Iwar. The term "houseboy" does not really describe the relationship between Iwar and Nancy. Iwar was with Nancy for nineteen years and cared for the house and saw to her needs through all of the years that she was in

Nigeria. When she took a new assignment in another location, Iwar considered it his assignment, too, and picked up the household goods and put them down in the new house.

"Iwar, use this broom," instructed Nancy. At first, she had to suggest many things that would speed up his house-keeping skills. "This is an American broom. I brought it from the States for you to use. Take it and use it. It will sweep better than the one you are using."

Iwar was not too sure of this, but did as Nancy asked, never becoming indignant in the face of instruction. He was a very handsome young man, of medium build with very black skin and a ready smile for Nancy's guests. He kept her house clean with the American broom and made sure that her clothes were washed and ironed. Everything was neat and tidy before he left for his own home each night.

Because Iwar was Nancy's employee and her houseboy, she was responsible for his well-being and his family's secu-rity, as well. She made sure that he had proper health care, built a house for him, and supervised the education of his two children. Iwar had married three times in the nineteen years that he worked for Nancy. His cooking skills became more than adequate and Nancy's house was always known for the abundance of food he prepared for her and any unexpected friends that came to her house. Nancy's coffee pot was always ready. He was loyal and dependable, freeing Nancy from routine house cares so that she could give all of her energies to the teaching of the Tiv young people.

Early in 1978, Nancy began to experience a different kind of emotion. Nancy, herself, called it "burn out." For the first time, she wondered if she had lost her effectiveness in Nigeria and if it was time for her to go home.

Iwar was her responsibility in Nigeria. He was her concern and the students at Teacher's College were her concern. She knew that she could not leave until her responsibilities were fulfilled. But Nancy was too firm in her faith to think that this was her decision to make. As she had done so often in her life since she had become God's child, Nancy went to the Lord on her knees and asked for His decision.

"Lord, I am tired. I don't feel effective in what I am doing. Is it time to let someone else take over this position, or do you want me to remain? Lord," Nancy continued, "Iwar needs an education, but he does not have the ability that others who have applied to Teacher's College possess. Make a way for him in this education field and I will know that he can take care of himself and that I have not deserted him. If this happens, I will know that You send me home to Michigan with Your blessing. I am receptive to Your will, Lord, and will obey Your commands."

Nancy talked to Iwar about her desire to return to her home in the States.

"I want to see you firmly established, Iwar, and I want to be assured that all will be well with you before I leave. You have helped me so faithfully these past nineteen years. I am deeply indebted to you and will miss you and all of my Nigerian friends here in Africa if the Lord confirms my plan to return home." Nancy looked at the face that was saddened by this news. "My hope is that you understand my reason for going, Iwar. That is very important to me."

Once more the Lord gave Nancy an answer. Against all odds, Iwar was admitted to Teacher's College to study for a ministry in teaching.

Iwar was overjoyed, but he realized at the same time that he was losing a very valuable friend as Nancy Chapel made plans to return to the United States, having served her Lord with all of her heart, mind and soul, with only the glory of God uppermost in her mind. She had faithfully brought her expertise and her love to the people of Nigeria. She had served her Lord well. Nancy Chapel could certainly claim the scripture as her own that said, "Well done, thou good and faithful servant."

Nancy returned to the United States on July 19, 1978. It was hard to say goodbye to all her Nigerian friends and colleagues in that land. It was difficult to say farewell to Iwar and his wife and children. But Nancy had asked the Lord to make the decision and He did just that.

Nancy had served Him faithfully, and it was time to move on to the next phase of her life and service to Him. She left, assured of His blessing.

11

HOME

HOME. A word that usually suggests comfort and safety. To a degree this has been true for Nancy Chapel in all of the places that she has called "home."

In the Ukraine growing up, home meant a place of refuge, a place to be sheltered from the grim reality of famine, Communist cruelty and the evil devices of men. At that time, home meant a place where brother and sister were cared for and nourished by a never-tiring mother, Oksana, who did the best she could to maintain the body and soul of a family.

Nadia had found another home where Geesken Gulker maintained a family in Germany, which was supposed to be her enemy's house. It turned out far different. This house in Germany, these strange people, became a cherished home for Nadia. It was in this setting that the Lord put His hand upon her life and drew this unbelieving young Ukrainian girl to Himself.

As Nancy Chapel, she established another home, a home in the United States, firmly attached to the church of her Lord and nourished by the people who with her proclaimed Him as Lord and Savior. In Grand Rapids, she had studied, improved her abilities to teach, earned a degree in education, and opened herself to the will of God for the rest of her life.

Her home had also been in Nigeria for almost twenty years. God chose this home for her and these people became like family to her. She was a part of them in mind and in spirit, and Nancy saw Nigeria with the heart of a native Tiv in Zaki Biam, Uavande, Harga and Mkar. She loved them and they returned her love with honor and gratitude.

Now, in 1978, Nancy had returned to her home in the United States. She would retire here and make her permanent residence with her dear friends from her church, her mission field associates, and a few special friends who had been faithfully corresponding with her during the years that she lived in Nigeria. Nancy Chapel was home.

"I bring you greetings from your many friends in Nigeria." These words were spoken by the woman in the pulpit at Mayfair Christian Reformed Church. This was Nancy Chapel and she had come forward at Rev. Witte's invitation to address the congregation. She wanted to thank the congregation for their love, for the many prayers uttered in her behalf, and for the support in numerous other ways during the twenty years that she had been their missionary and friend.

"My dress that I wear today was made for me and given to me by my friends in Nigeria, as well as the matching head-dress. It is a dress that would be worn for a special occasion and they wanted me to have it as a farewell gift."

The dress was a beautiful green print, full length in the native Tiv style, with the headdress made like a turban and placed smartly on Nancy's head. "They did this as a gift of love to me, and I wear it today as a tribute to you from me and all of your Nigerian brothers and sisters in Christ in Nigeria. From the bottom of my heart, I thank you for your love. I think of you as 'my love family' here at Mayfair. I will be living here in Grand Rapids now and working at Blodgett Hospital. It is good to be home. God bless you!"

"It's so good to have you home, Nancy," declared Fran Bratt, who with her family was also back home from Nigeria. "But I wonder, Nancy, have you thought any-more about going back to the Ukraine to find your own family?"

"Not yet, Fran. Not yet."

Nancy moved into an apartment in Grand Rapids and kept herself busy working, teaching Bible lessons for societies and being a faithful worker at church, visiting the sick and talking with those who needed a friend. She had retired, but had not given up the Lord's ministry. She had just switched her place of operation.

Her friend, Jenny Sytsma, who was a German girl who had come to the United States as the adopted daughter of the Diekjacobs family in Holland and who had corresponded so faithfully with Nancy in Nigeria, enjoyed a renewed friendship with Nancy. As the years went by, they became close friends. Gerry VandenBerg was also home from Nigeria, and she and Nancy had many opportunities to share news about their friends in Nigeria.

In the early 1990s, changes occurred in the government structure in the Ukraine and the power of the Communist party was crushed. Russia was becoming more receptive to foreigners traveling in their country. So the question of another "home" confronted Nancy once again. The Ukraine was her birthplace, but the United States was her chosen home. Still, she had a need to go and see if she could find any of her relatives in Soldativ.

"Maybe this is the time to go," thought Nancy.

Her friend Jenny wanted to go to Russia with her. So did Fran Karnamaat, a missionary colleague of Nancy's from Nigeria. Alida Terpstra also expressed a desire to make the trip and so the four women proceeded to make plans to travel to the Ukraine to find Nancy's family.

It was not that easy. There were passports to be applied for, visas to be obtained from the Soviet government. They even needed a letter of invitation from someone in the country before the visas would be issued. It was expensive to make such a trip and Nancy would need help financially. As in all things, Nancy prayed about the trip and asked the Lord to help her to make it possible to go, if it was His will.

Once the news was out that Nancy had this in mind, the support started coming in. Friends who wanted a part of this adventure for Nancy gave her money and encouragement. The Sunday School children at Mayfair had a pie sale and gave Nancy the proceeds.

Finally, when the tickets were actually purchased, Nancy went into her own kind of action. Each of the women could take two suitcases with them on the plane.

Nancy asked them to put their things in only one and give her the other piece of luggage to pack things to take to her family and friends in the Ukraine.

Everything that Nancy thought would be useful was in those suitcases. Her apartment looked like the back room of a department store. In the end, it took a pair of pliers to close the suitcases and, hopefully, they would never be opened until they were in the U.S.S.R.

"Alida, I can't believe that we are actually going," shared Nancy, as the two women stood looking at the packed luggage in Nancy's living room.

"Well, you might not be going unless you have someone to help with these suitcases. They are so heavy, I couldn't move them an inch to go by to the bathroom!" exclaimed her friend. "I just climbed over them!"

"I know, but Harvey Bratt said he would come to help us the day of our flight."

Nancy was quiet for a minute. Her dear friend, Fran Bratt, Harvey's wife, who had always encouraged her to go back to the Ukraine, had gone to be with the Lord two weeks earlier after a long struggle with cancer.

"I wish Fran were here to share my joy," responded Nancy. "She would have been so pleased that I am finally going back to settle that issue for good."

"I'm sure she knows, Nancy. She is with her Lord, now. Her joy is complete." Alida looked at her friend and saw that there were tears in Nancy's eyes, and in hers as well.

All of the last minute preparations were done and at long last Nancy was ready to go back to the Ukraine. She had no idea where they would stay in Kiev or how they would get to the small village of Soldativ. She was traveling in faith that the Lord would show her the way and take care of the four American women in a strange country.

As Nancy struggled to get finished, she had a phone call from a friend who urged her to come to a meeting where a woman from the Ukraine would also attend.

"Oh no, I'm so busy. There isn't time," responded Nancy.

But, in the end she went. She met Olga Ajay who had a sister living in Kiev.

"I will call my sister and tell her that you are coming. She will meet you, I know, and see that you have a place to stay. Don't worry, I will take care of it."

Such welcome words from a stranger. Would she arrange it all for Nancy?

"We'll see," thought Nancy. "It would be

an answer to prayer if her sister did meet us at the airport in Kiev."

The last night in Grand Rapids before the long-awaited departure to the Ukraine, Nancy tried in vain to sleep. After several hours of tossing and turning, she finally got out of bed and stood by the living-room window looking out at the lights of the city glowing in a cloudless sky.

She thought of the possibilities that lay ahead of her. It was hard to believe that she was actually going to the Ukraine tomorrow.

"Without my 'love family' this trip would not be possible," mused Nancy. "How can I ever thank my friends and the members of Mayfair Church for all their support? And those dear children in the Sunday School class. I can still see their eager faces as they gave me the money that they earned at that bake sale for me! Such precious lambs of God!

"I have been in many places and situations in my life; some I welcomed, some I didn't. But they were all from God for His purpose and His Kingdom work, even though I was not even aware of His plans for me. If He had asked me if I wanted to lead that kind of life, I would have said 'No. Let me do it my way. Let me plan my own life.' But He had a different plan.

Just think of all of the blessings that I would have missed had He not opened my eyes so that I could see Him and He had not cleansed my heart of hatred and distrust, so that I could follow His lead."

Nancy sighed as she stood in the dark, slowly reviewing the events of her life. And now, in God's care, she was ready to go back to the Ukraine to look for her family.

"I am so blessed!" thought Nancy. "The humiliation and suffering of my childhood and youth paved the way for me to understand other people's needs, and God gave me the ability to use this understanding to help others and bring them closer to the love of Jesus Christ.

"Now I can see that those hate-filled people in the Ukraine and Hitler's men in Germany meant it for evil, but God turned it all to His glory. Only a loving Heavenly Father could accomplish that."

With tears in her eyes, Nancy remembered the words of a hymn that had meant so much to her:

"My heart cries out:
'My God, how wonderful You are,
*   Your majesty how bright!*
How beautiful Your mercy seat
*   in depths of burning light.*
No earthly father loves like you . . .
*   Yet I may love you, too!'"*

Nancy's sister Maria, 1992.

*Nancy with tribute bread
at farewell celebration.*

EPILOGUE

Nancy Chapel did make the long-awaited trip to the Ukraine with her three friends. After much trouble with the overloaded suitcases, they finally arrived at the Borispol Airport in Kiev. To their delight, Katya Filonenko was there to meet them. Olga Ajay had indeed kept her promise and contacted her sister in Kiev.

Katya and her husband, Vladimir, took charge of the group, housing them in their small apartment and helping Nancy arrange to go back to her birthplace of Soldativ.

Making the trip from Kiev to Soldativ was difficult, as roads were poor; but the reward at the end in Sodativ made it all worthwhile. Villagers came out into the road to see the unexpected strangers, to talk and to find out who they were. Nancy saw her cottage by the side of the pond, facing the opposite way this time. It had burned and the present owner had rebuilt it. The older people in the village told Nancy that her brother Boris' daughter, Katya Chaplya, lived in nearby Petrovka-

Romenska. And, miracle of all miracles, Maria, Nancy's older sister, lived with her there! Her brother Boris had died some years earlier of cancer.

After a tearful reunion, Nancy and Maria spent many hours talking and trying to fill in the gap of fifty years. They talked about the good times and the cruel times, about families and friends, deaths and marriages. They laughed and cried.

Nancy learned that her father, Anton Chaplya, had been released after some years from the work prison in Siberia and had returned to the village of Soldativ, living out his remaining years with his wife, Oksana. "He died when he was 82, in 1969, and our mother lived until 1972," she was told.

The gifts that Nancy and the other women distributed were much appreciated. Life had been hard for Maria. Nancy conveyed to Maria the joy that she had found in Jesus Christ, and how fulfilled she was to be His servant.

Every day, Nancy had her personal devotions and Maria always was there to listen. "If you are so religious, Nadia, why don't you wear a cross around your neck?" asked Maria.

"I have no need of a cross on a chain, Maria. I have the love of the Lord in my heart, and that is enough."

Side by side, the Chaplya sisters strolled the narrow roads of their birthplace and greeted the neighbors as they came out of their houses to see them. The days went swiftly, and as the time of good-byes approached, Maria began to worry about the coming separation.

"How can I let you go?" asked Maria. "Now that I have found you again, how can I let you leave me? Stay here, Nadia."

"No, Maria, your home is here and mine is in Michigan. I must return to my work and to whatever the Lord has for me to accomplish in His name. But we must give God the glory and praise for bringing us together."

Maria and Nancy made one last trip to Soldativ together to visit the graves of their parents. As the sisters stood there side by side, Nancy knew that now she could go back home with peace in her heart. The Lord had given her the opportunity to meet with her blood family in the Ukraine and be a "pointer" for them toward salvation, freedom from fear and mistrust, and ultimate peace in heaven with Jesus Christ.

"I am so blessed," thought Nancy. "The humiliation and suffering of my childhood and youth paved the way to understanding of other people's suffering and needs, and God gave me the ability to use this understanding to help others think and care about their suffering without bitterness and resentment. Only a living God could accomplish that! Only *He* could use people who were my enemies, who forced the separation of me from my family and who compelled me to work for them in a foreign country, as an instrument to point to the freedom of the soul and membership in the family of God, show me how to live without fear, hate and darkness, and supply me with a joyful life in eternity. What is not possible with man *is* possible with God!"

This book was produced by the Christian Literature Crusade. We hope it has been helpful to you in living the Christian life. CLC is a literature mission with ministry in over 40 countries worldwide. If you would like to know more about us, or are interested in opportunities to serve with a faith mission, we invite you to write to:

Christian Literature Crusade
P.O. Box 1449
Fort Washington, PA 19034